ALL THINGS
IN TIME

ALL THINGS
IN TIME

SUE BUYER

atmosphere press

*Dedicated to Liz, without whose help
this book never would have seen the light of day.*

Book One

Prologue

It was a very different time. Five years after the end of World War II, many of the veterans who had finished college under the GI Bill dreamt of a house in the suburbs, a stay-at-home wife and four or five well-behaved children.

There were magazine ads that encouraged those dreams. One showed a smiling young woman in high-heeled shoes pushing a vacuum cleaner. Another depicted a smiling housewife hugging rolls of toilet paper.

This is the story of two women who didn't buy into that picture.

The first was Nina Silver, who'd been hired as a temporary general assignment reporter at *The Buffalo Evening Gazette*. The second was Betty Roeder, working then as a checkout clerk in a new supermarket. While their stories would intertwine over decades, they met only once.

The story begins the Monday after Thanksgiving in 1950. The day before, nine inches of snow had fallen. Most of it still lay there. The plows that could have cleared that snow overnight had not yet been connected to the trucks that power them.

Twenty-three-year-old Nina Silver, who lived within a mile of the newspaper offices, had made it to work that snowy November 26th in her warmest coat, ski hat and heavy boots. Nina remembered the story of Buffalo Congressman Hank Nowak, who, it was rumored, had been the only member of Congress to reach his office after an unexpected, heavy Washington, DC snowstorm. She wanted to show her new employers that she was just as hardy.

In her few months at the paper, Nina had done little but write obituaries and fifty-word "city briefs." That wasn't what she'd hoped her job would be.

Chapter 1
THE ASSIGNMENT
1950

Miles away and earlier that morning, two hunters had telephoned the Cattaraugus County sheriff to tell him that as they set out that morning, they had found the body of a tiny infant in an otherwise empty lidded plastic pumpkin, abandoned near the start of their path into the woods. At first, they assumed some child had lost his trick-or-treat loot in what must have been a heavy wind on Halloween, the month before. Expecting to find frozen candy, they lifted the lid and peeked inside. They were shocked to find the body of a tiny infant wearing diapers and a shirt. There was no question that the infant was dead and had been for a while. Stunned, they stood for half a minute and then quickly agreed to drive back to the last store they had passed, a pharmacy about a mile back. They had to ask what county they were in before they knew what sheriff to call.

The sheriff, John Simpson, always looking for publicity, then called the *Buffalo Gazette* before setting out to the scene. Al Mrozak, the Western New York editor of the *Gazette*, called the darkroom and talked to photographer Mike O'Neill, the first photographer who had made it in to the office that morning. Mrozak instructed him to go to the site and take a reporter along. Like all the photographers, he had snow tires on his car.

"Mike, I need you to drive down to Cattaraugus County. Take that new reporter, whose name I can never remember, with you. I hope she can handle this. She's only done obits, city briefs and the garden club column since she came, but she's all I've got here now. The story can't wait until someone experienced comes in. We'll fill in later. She can get us a paragraph or two. I want those photos ASAP. Take the one *Gazette* car with the telephone."

"Okay. Just where am I going?" Mike asked.

"Two hunters found an infant's dead body early this morning in the woods near South Dayton. Get a map. Call the sheriff's office for directions. Find the place. Get going and take that girl with you. Silver. I think that's her name. Let's hope she doesn't faint when she sees a body."

Then Mrozak called Nina to his desk. "Silver," he yelled as she was taking off her coat. Maybe, she hoped, she'd be given an interesting assignment because so few people were in the office that day.

"Yes, sir," the five-foot-two, curly haired brunette in the heavy ski sweater responded.

City editor Mrozak explained to Nina, "Two deer hunters found a baby's body in the woods this morning just after dawn. Their hike into the rural Cattaraugus County hills came to a halt when one of them spotted a large plastic pumpkin wedged against the limb of a fallen tree. They picked it up, lifted the lid and were horrified to find the body of a tiny infant.

"I'm sending you out with Mike O'Neill, one of our photographers, on what may be this baby's murder. It has to be a quick turnaround. O'Neill will get pictures of the site where they found the body. I need his photos as soon as humanly possible. Get what more you can from the cop at the site while Mike shoots pictures. Talk to anyone you can and describe what you learned. I'll get more details later when someone else gets here. What I need from you is the available information. Take anything the cops will tell you. The hunters, I gather, went farther into the woods as soon as the police arrived.

"I just need a few paragraphs. This paper has one car with a phone. Mike will drive it today. There's nobody else here yet, and I need this story ASAP. Since driving may be slow, I want you to phone in as Mike drives back. Have you got boots?"

"Yes, sir. I walked to work this morning in boots and a long, warm toggle coat."

Chapter 2
THE RIDE

Nina had not been on an assignment with Mike O'Neill before or really noticed him. He was a good ten inches taller than she—young, brown eyes, brown hair. Cute, she thought.

The trip down took over an hour and the two made small talk. "You sound like you're from New York. Are you?" she asked.

"Yup. Born and raised in upper Manhattan. Graduate of Regis High School, the number-one-ranked Catholic high school in all of Manhattan. Someday, I hope to get back to the Big Apple and have a good job there. In the meantime, I have no complaints here. You a Buffalo native?"

"Yes, still living at home. How long have you been at the *Gazette*, Mike?"

"Two years. I take it you just came this summer."

"Yes. I'm one of the three who started in June. Tom Johnson, Bob Peterson and me."

"Recent graduate, I presume."

"Yes. Peterson and I finished at Columbia. I don't know where Johnson came from. My guess is that his diploma is as new as ours."

That ended the conversation and they rode the rest of the way in silence.

By the time they arrived, the body had been removed

from the site. Sheriff John Simpson was still there.

"What can you tell us?" Nina asked.

"Female, age about three weeks, according to the medical examiner. No ID. Babies don't carry drivers' licenses, you know. All I've got is this tiny piece of print fabric that was caught in the top fold of the baby's diaper."

"Are you going to photograph the fabric and try to match it?" Nina asked the sheriff.

"Well, little Sherlock Holmes," he said sarcastically. "No. Even, if we were to spend weeks finding where it came from, it was probably used for seven hundred dresses and maybe dozens were sold around here.

"We'll solve this case when the baby's parents show up. The fact that no one has reported a missing baby around here probably means that the parents are away and left the kid with a none-too-reliable sitter. Or, maybe they aren't from around here. Maybe they couldn't stand the baby's crying and did her in. Stranger things have happened."

Mike got a couple of shots of the sheriff standing near the plastic pumpkin in the snow. Nina noted its size and the distance into the woods. She put it all together and dictated a short piece as soon as they got back to the car.

They started the ride back in depressed silence. Then, they briefly discussed the tragedy. Mike eventually turned on the car radio, moving the dial away from police reports to a popular music station. The voice of Tony Bennett singing "Stranger in Paradise" rang through the car. Mike joined in singing after a bit. Then Nina did too. Her voice was not as good as his, but she sang away. Next came Dean Martin singing "That's Amore." Unexpectedly, there was a shot of electricity between the two.

Sensing it, Mike turned off the radio and paid full attention to the road ahead. Nina sensed it too. She wondered whether Mike was single and whether the paper had rules about employee dating. She'd been going with a young resident physician who seemed only able to talk about tired he was.

Back at the office, Mike went straight to the darkroom. Nina spent the afternoon at her usual assignments, checking on who had died and writing fifty-word briefs. When the grey-haired, overweight reporter Dick Truesdale came in, he was given the baby story. He checked what Nina had written and picked up the phone to see if the Cattaraugus County Sheriff had more to tell. He saw no reason to walk across the newsroom and talk to Nina. That bothered her. She hadn't spent a postgraduate year in journalism school to write obituaries. She had thought this trip would show the editor that she could handle real news. In any case, she had been glad to get out of the grey-walled office with its grey desks on this grey day.

Chapter 3
MUCH ADO ABOUT NOTHING

Nina was hopeful that after her work on Friday she would get a decent assignment on Monday, at least covering a meeting or conducting interviews for a feature. She picked up her assignment envelope for the day and her face fell.

There were two death notices from local undertakers hoping the deceased would be found interesting enough for an obituary. There was also a two-page handwritten letter about a church Christmas concert with directions from an assistant city editor to rewrite it in fifty words.

Frowning, Nina started walking toward her desk when she heard Mrozak yell out "Silver!" across the newsroom. He was holding a telephone away from his ear. As soon as she approached his desk, he said, "Take this call. It has to do with your story Friday about that baby's body in the pumpkin shell."

Nina hurried into one of the phone booths lining a wall of the newsroom to keep conversations private. Mrozak leaned over to the rewrite man sitting across from him and said softly, "Let's see how she deals with this."

The woman on the phone was talking as fast as she could. "Your story yesterday—that's my baby. Her father, my ex-husband, kidnapped her. Now I'm afraid he's murdered her. He said he was taking her to the zoo, but I never saw either of them again. It's been almost two years."

As excited as she was to be working on a real story, Nina knew something was wrong. Neither an infant's body nor a plastic pumpkin would have lasted through two Western New York winters, and why would someone take a three-week-old infant to the zoo?

"How old was your daughter when she vanished?" Nina said in as normal a voice as she could.

"I'd separated from that no-good husband. It was just before the baby's fourth birthday. On my own, I had a party already planned. The jerk came by a few days before. He had visiting rights, because the judge was a moron. I shouldn't have let him take her. I've been frantic ever since, and now your story confirmed my worst fears and tells me that he killed her."

"I hope you find your daughter alive and well someday," Nina said softly, "but this baby was only a few weeks old. The body in that plastic pumpkin was tiny."

"My daughter was small for her age," the woman volunteered.

"I'm so sorry. I have read that fathers seldom kill their children after kidnapping them. Give me your name and telephone number, and if we ever hear anything, we'll call you."

A crestfallen Nina walked over to the city desk. "I'm sure you knew that wasn't the missing mother."

"Well somebody had to talk to her. It was good experience for you. Who knows? We may get a real call yet. You did a good job talking to that woman. I'll let you take other calls on the subject if they come in."

But as time passed, there never was another call about the pumpkin infant.

Years would go by. The case would be forgotten,

although it remained in the cold-case file in the sheriff's office and in Nina's memory. The fact that no one ever came forward rankled in her mind. Nina would always remember it as the first real story of her newspaper career. It was the only murder she would ever cover.

In the early 1950s, women reporters were almost never sent on assignments involving murders or accidents. In fact, one New Year's Eve afternoon a few years later, when no one was in the office except for the three women reporters, a plane crashed sixty miles south of the city. Nina heard Mrozak phone one of his top male reporters and say, "There's been a plane crash near Salamanca, south of the city. I have no one here. I'm sorry to do this, but I need you to come in to work."

If covering murders and accidents had been routine, maybe Nina would have forgotten about the baby in the pumpkin. Because it turned out to be a once-in-a-lifetime experience, she never did. In fact, she always hoped that someday she would help solve the mystery.

Chapter 4
THE WORTH

The week following the Cattaraugus County trip, Mike called Nina.

"A group of us from the paper go out for drinks after work on Saturdays. We gather at the bar in the Worth Hotel next door to the paper. Care to join us? After a drink or two, other than the guys who go home to wives and kids, the rest of us usually head to Montgomery's for steak."

Nina could not have assented more quickly. When Saturday rolled around, since they'd both driven to work, they each drove their own cars to Dan Montgomery's Restaurant after the drinks at the old hotel.

The restaurant on Exchange Street was just outside the busy downtown in a decaying industrial area. It was never crowded, perhaps because the forty-five-year-old wooden tables and chairs looked every bit their age—or more. There was always room to park and a good-size steak plate could be had for six dollars. It was a hangout for the reporters and was less than a mile from the newsroom.

The Saturday "beer jaunt" became a weekly thing for Nina and Mike. There was no Sunday paper. Only one desk man had to show up Sunday morning to take calls about accidents, shootings and fires. No one else came to work until afternoon.

Saturday evening, therefore, was a celebration and a

critique time for the week that was. Nina quickly became an active participant at these get-togethers. As the weeks went by, she often, but not always, sat next to Mike. Everyone talked, sometimes all at once.

Other than the Saturdays at the Worth and sometimes at Dan Montgomery's with the group, Nina rarely saw Mike except in passing at the paper. Photographers and reporters seldom traveled together unless a story was in one of the seven outlying counties the *Gazette* considered its circulation area. A reporter sometimes spent an hour on an interview; the photographer could finish in under ten minutes. So, if the mileage wasn't great, they went to the assignment separately. Mike and Nina rarely had the same assignment, but they had begun going to the movies together from time to time after the group sessions at the Worth and Montgomery's.

One afternoon the following winter, they were given a joint assignment near Arcade, forty-two miles south of the city. An Arcade Central schoolteacher of what was then called Home Economics had written an article to be published in *Women's Day* magazine. Her thesis was that the color of interior walls affected the mood of a home's residents. She insisted that kitchen walls should always be yellow to keep diners in good spirits. Mike had talked with the woman on the phone to set up the time and date before Nina was assigned to the story.

"I think this woman is a handful. I asked if a reporter with a photographer could interview her during her free period. She said she used that time for meditation. She turned down a Saturday interview because it would interfere with her errands. The only time she was willing to be photographed and interviewed was after school at three-thirty in her classroom."

The sky was grey, but the weather was dry when Nina and Mike left the newsroom for Arcade. As they headed south, it began to snow, gradually growing heavier the farther south of the city they drove.

"You know," Mike said, growing talkative during the drive, "being a news photographer is not my ambition in life. I want to do fashion shoots and portraits. That's where you can take the time to do a really great job and that's where the big money is.

"I've taken portraits of Margaret Lowell, the wife of one of the vice presidents of Marine Midland, and Betty Cooper, the former checkout clerk who just married the owner of the grocery store where she worked. My portfolio of portraits is in the folder on the back seat. I think you can reach over and get it, if you are interested." Nina wiggled around, got the folder and opened it.

She pulled out the top photo. It was a picture of a pretty, blonde woman. Nina gasped. "The dress that woman is wearing matches the scrap of fabric caught in that dead baby's diaper that they found last November. Maybe she was involved!"

"That photo is of Betty Cooper of Cooper's Market. Your idea is a little far-fetched, don't you think? Maybe three hundred women have the same dress," he said. "Maybe three thousand. On the very slim chance that there is even a connection, I doubt they could prove it based on matching the fabric in the diaper with the print on this woman's dress."

"I'm not convinced. I'm going to call that sheriff first thing Monday morning," Nina announced.

"Think about this," Mike said. "Do you really imagine

that the sheriff will go up to Mrs. Cooper and tell her that, since she owned a dress like one maybe worn by a perhaps murderer, would she like to confess to that crime? Anyway, my photo is in black and white. Her dress may have been a different color. Forget about it, please. What did the sheriff call you, 'Junior Sherlock Holmes'?"

No more was said on the subject, but Nina fumed about the condescending comment for the remaining fifty minutes of the long ride. They made it to the school, which was just a few miles out of Arcade in Yorkville. It took longer than expected to find the right classroom, because they wasted time looking for the home economics department in the nearly deserted school building. They found one basketball player leaving the school. When they asked him where the Home Ec department was, he looked at Mike as though he'd asked how to get to outer space. "Haven't an inkling," the young man responded as he hurried out the door.

Because of the time lost in wandering the empty corridors and the length of time it took to get more information from the teacher, who was reluctant to tell how she got interested in wall color, it was close to five when they left the building.

The snowfall had grown heavier. Mike turned on the car radio.

"Heavy snowstorm in the south towns," the announcer intoned. "Routes 39 and 62 are closed. If you're trying to get home, use the back roads. If you're not already in your car, it's best to stay where you are until the heavy snow lets up, probably in a few hours." Mike said nothing, turned off the radio and stayed at the wheel.

"I bet we can get through," he said.

After half an hour and less than half a mile in a whiteout, he gave up. "No way. There's a hotel in town. I've never been in it, but I know it's here. We'll get a couple of rooms, have dinner, spend the night, get up at the crack of dawn and be safely back in Buffalo by the time my early shift begins."

When they tried to check in, the clerk said sharply, "You want two rooms? No way. By early evening, folks will be sleeping on the lobby floor. You can, however, have a room with two beds." Mike nodded at Nina. She shrugged and agreed.

"We'll have a drink and a leisurely dinner and then watch TV," Mike said as they opened the door to the plain but clean room.

"You'd better phone down and make that dinner reservation immediately. Let them know we're guests in the hotel. People seem to be arriving every minute," Nina said.

They asked for a table right away because the bar was jammed. Like the dozen people ahead of them, they had to wait. The line in front of them, however, was shorter than the line growing behind them. It looked like it would be a long evening.

When they got back to the room, Nina called home to explain to her parents why she would not be home that night. "We've got rooms in a hotel in Arcade," she said, thinking how one little "s" on rooms evaded the truth.

Mike turned on the television. There was Thursday Night Wrestling, which appealed to neither of them. Nor did "Famous Jury Trials." They settled on The Kraft Theater offering, but it made no sense to them, as it was halfway over before they got back to the room and because they had each had a couple of drinks.

"I guess I should keep a deck of cards in my glove compartment," Mike muttered.

He wandered about the small room and announced "Hey, if you are chilly, there is an extra blanket in the closet. You can have it."

"We could push the beds together and throw the blanket over the top of both of us," Nina suggested.

"If I weren't a gentleman, I'd suggest a better way of keeping warm," Mike volunteered with a grin.

"You know, I've been wondering why you have never made a pass at me over all these months," said the slightly tipsy Nina. "I have to admit, when we're together, my heart beats faster. I've hoped it was the same for you."

"Well, now that you mention it, I thought about it, but I didn't follow through. Not because I didn't want to but because we often work together. Getting close would be easy but breaking up could be a real problem," Mike said.

"We're here. We're not going out until morning. I don't want to shock you, but, since we both seem interested, why not a one-night fling? No reminiscing about it tomorrow. No regrets," Nina said.

"Lovely idea but bad idea," Mike said.

"What's the harm?" Nina asked.

"I've dreamed more than once about taking you in my arms," Mike answered. "It would be a lovely way to warm up on a wintry night," he continued, "but, it's a bad idea for coworkers to get involved."

"We wouldn't have to go all the way," Nina said softly. "If it were your idea, it would have taken me about four seconds to jump at the invitation. We didn't plan to run off to this hotel room, but here we are. Blame snow or fate."

"I feel like the devil is singing in my ear," Mike said. "But we're both adults. If we agreed ahead on only a one-night stand, it might help me get over my obsession with you. It's something we both want. What would be the harm? We could tell ourselves that it's just because we need to share a blanket. Of course, neither of us would believe that and no one else needs to ever know."

With that, he had her in his arms.

"Every Saturday, when I've sat beside you at the Worth, I've pretended that shock of electricity didn't happen," Nina said. "Now I'm admitting that it certainly did."

"I have to admit I feel the same way," Mike answered. "I really want to get to know you better—in every sense of the word," he said with a grin. It's probably not something the *Gazette* would approve of, but my guess is that romance is showing its head no matter how we push it back down."

"Look, we're in a hotel room where no one will walk in on us. Why not let it happen? If this were a movie with two single adults and a bed, no one would complain about a missing deck of cards," Nina said with a sly look.

"Fate brought us here. We didn't plan on the snowstorm. Who am I to argue with that that?" Mike asked. After a very few moments, they stopped talking. The night flew by quickly.

The next morning, when the five o'clock wake-up call that Mike had requested came, both groaned. Mike grinned. Nina allowed, "Well this has to be one of my more enjoyable assignments. I've been hoping for quite some time something would develop between us. I'm glad it did. What is it that people say? 'Whatever will be, will be'?"

"What will be is that right now we've got to wipe the

snow off our car and the grins off our faces," Mike said. He went to the window and saw that the lot had been plowed.

"I am going to clean off the car. You can take ten more minutes, but then we have to get going. I don't want to repeat the mistake I once made after a snowstorm. That night, I spent ten minutes clearing snow off the wrong car. This time I counted the parking spaces. But first, if I can open the hotel window, I want a picture of this parking lot. It looks like a row of frosted Hostess cupcakes waiting for the coconut."

He gave her a kiss on the top of the head as he went toward the door. Nina followed shortly to help or at least to offer to help. As he brushed the snow from the windshield, Mike turned to Nina and said, "You know, we are going to have to be careful. We both agreed this was just one fun evening. We'll discuss it as we drive."

Once in the car, Mike began, "This was a night better than I could have imagined. Wow. But, that said, let's stick with our plan and keep things casual. It will all be so much easier that way."

Disappointment showed on Nina's face. The night's electricity had made her reconsider her suggestion that it be only a one-night stand. Still, she said nothing she might later regret.

Nina responded, "I'm not looking for a serious relationship at this point either. We did say it would be a one-night thing. Besides, I can't imagine what my mother would say if we developed something more serious. That said, it sure was great."

Chapter 5
NEW YORK?

Once back at work, Nina decided to wait for Mike to bring up their night in Arcade and hopefully make the next move. It was the following Sunday afternoon before he did. Although Nina lived with her parents, she had her own telephone line. She grinned when she heard Mike's voice on the phone.

"Got time for a cup of coffee this afternoon? I can drive over. There is something I need to tell you," he said.

"My folks are home, and my mother is always rude to any man other than the dull one she's set her heart on for me. If it is someone named O'Neill at the door, she'll be even ruder than usual. So, rather than meeting here, I'll meet you at the Howard Johnson's on Delaware Avenue for an ice-cream soda or anywhere you like," Nina volunteered.

"Ice cream in the middle of winter is not on my list of favorite things, but I'll meet anywhere you say. However, here's a suggestion: If I promise to behave, how about my apartment? Phil Denton, the movie critic who is my roommate, spends every weekend with his fiancé in Batavia. It's his hometown. I'm on the second floor of the yellow-brick house at 350 Bedford Avenue, right near Elmwood."

"I'll be there in about fifteen minutes. I'm guessing your news is that you neglected to tell me that you're engaged."

"Let's wait to talk until you get here," said Mike.

Nina was at Mike's door fifteen minutes later. After she took off her coat and accepted Mike's offer of a cup of black coffee, he launched right into his news.

"I'm not ready to tell the paper yet, but I want you to hear it from me. Please keep this between us. I'm moving back to New York. I've got a job at *Charm* magazine. They want me there before they start on their biggest issue of the year, the college one, and they need me to start sooner than I had expected. We've been talking for a while, but now it's official. To be precise, I am moving in eight weeks. With my new magazine job, I'll be able to spend more time on each photo and the pay will be significantly higher. In my spare time, I might even be able to begin the freelance work I have always wanted to do. I am really excited about this job.

"Of course, there is a downside. I know we both agreed that it was just a fling, but I know for me, and think it's true for you too, that whatever started between us was more than that. We sure had a great night, but it's about more than that. You are smart, attractive and fun to be around, so who knows? However, I'm not going to be here to see what could develop. And yet, I don't want to totally let this go. Hey, who knows, maybe in time, you too will get a great offer and will want to move to the big city. You are a good writer and my guess is that many single reporters are recruited from the smaller circulation papers, and, of course, it would be a great opportunity because it's where so much of the big news breaks."

Mike paused and then became serious. "However, for now, if word gets out that I'm leaving, the *Gazette* will say

"Leave today." I'll give them a month's notice, but I can't afford to spend two months unemployed, so I need your word that you won't say a thing. That brings me back to us. In the time that I am here, and despite what I would like, it would be neither kind nor ethical to take up your time. I wanted to talk to you today so you would understand the real reason why we can't get involved."

"Given the other night, I'd also like to spend more time with you—a lot more time," Nina responded. "But I agree with you. Those long-distance romances don't work, particularly ones that haven't been long-term local romances first. Oh, and I doubt that I will follow you. I've always wanted to be a reporter. I've got my dream chance here."

Nina went on, "I think I'm pretty good, but not good enough for the highly competitive New York market. If I somehow got a newspaper job there, it would be as a copy girl or a researcher. Let's just make some great memories before you leave. If that interests you, I'm game for making the most of the time we have here."

"I dreamt you drove to New York with me," Mike said. "Instead of an eight-hour trip, we took three days, stopping for overnight hotel stays in Rochester, Syracuse and Albany," he volunteered.

They were both quiet for a short time. Then, Nina spoke again.

"Hey, some people would say that a short, obligation-free romance is a dream come true. You once told me we're the same age—twenty-three. In my mind, that's way too young for anything permanent. Besides, my mother isn't very religious, but I'm an only child. I think she'd have a major fit if I ran off with a Catholic, which I presume you are."

"You sure can get carried away, but I like the way you think. Let's focus on the short term."

Nina knew her parents would be at a dinner party the next Saturday night, but just in case they were home early, as she left for the Worth that late afternoon, she told them she would probably be late coming home since one of the other reporters was having a party.

She told the same story the next week. This time, Nina's mother said, "I don't like you driving home alone late on a Saturday night. Why don't you bring your car home after the Worth and let someone else drive you to and from the party?"

"Good idea. I know just who I can ask," Nina volunteered.

"What's his name?" Hannah Silver asked.

"Mike O'Neill. He's a *Gazette* photographer who doesn't live too far from here."

"Sounds Catholic to me. Aren't there any single Jewish reporters at the newspaper who could drive you home?"

"It's just a ride to and from a party. I'm not eloping," Nina retorted and out the door she went.

Nina and Mike found ways to spend time alone together as often as they could over the next few weeks. Saying goodbye was even more difficult than either had expected; they had fallen for each other. At the very end of April, after Mike moved and his photo bylines disappeared from the paper, Mrs. Silver breathed a sigh of relief but she said nothing.

Chapter 6
THE GIRL NEXT DOOR
1951

Now back in New York, Mike had Sunday dinners with his family. They were often joined for dessert by their long-time next-door neighbors, a family with two sons and a daughter, Caitlin, just a year younger than Mike. He'd always regarded her as the younger sister he'd never had. He shared her joy six months earlier when she was invited to join the year-old Brooklyn Quartet when its second violinist left to join the Baltimore Philharmonic. The group had already committed to a full calendar of bookings, particularly after Bruce Williams, the first violinist, won the international Sibelius Violin Competition in Finland.

The second night Mike was back in New York, his family and Caitlin's had dinner together. After the chicken and the apple pie, Caitlin whispered to Mike. "I've got to talk to you."

It was a lovely spring evening and the two families smiled at each other when the young people went for their post-dinner walk. Both sets of parents had always hoped that the friendship between Mike and Caitlin would lead to romance and they grinned at the departure.

Once Mike and Caitlin were out of earshot of their parents, Caitlin announced:

"I'm in love. I can't tell my parents. Bruce is the first violinist in our quartet. He's married but he's getting a divorce. He's been separated for a year. His wife now lives in California. My parents will have a fit about me dating a divorced man."

"Congratulations, I think. I am very happy for you, " Mike said and then he paused. After a beat, he said, "Not to rain on your parade, but that 'getting a divorce' is an old story. It has led many a young woman astray. Are you absolutely sure about the divorce? Has he told you exactly when this is going to happen?"

"I know how it sounds," Caitlin said. "But he really is in the process of getting a divorce. His wife couldn't stand his traveling. She's moved to Los Angeles. They have no kids. I didn't know him well at school because he was two years ahead of me, but I always admired him from a distance. Since I joined the quartet, I have really gotten to know him, and we have spent a lot quality time together."

"Okay," said Mike, "I am really happy for you.–But promise me, Caitlin, that you will be careful. Maybe his story is true. Then maybe it isn't. I'm just looking out for you."

Chapter 7
THE ELOPEMENT

On Thursdays and Fridays, Mike worked a late shift but he was back in his folks' house the evening Caitlin returned from a midwestern tour with the quartet. She called him as soon as she got back in town. It was a rainy day, so rather than take a walk, they agreed to meet at Finnegan's, the corner bar near their houses. When they met at the door, Caitlin asked for the quiet booth in the back, the one that offered maximum privacy. She was not smiling.

"Always good to see you. You know that. But you look troubled. What's up?"

"Mike, are you engaged or in a serious relationship?"

Somewhat puzzled by the question, he said, "No. Odd way to start a conversation. Why do you ask?" Nina had been to visit one long weekend. They'd had fun, but it was nothing too serious.

As soon as they sat down, Caitlin looked at Mike and quietly announced, "Mike, I'm pregnant. Bruce's divorce won't come through for a few more months. It's a nightmare. Our audiences are often school kids. As I am a single woman, when my pregnancy begins to show, it will ruin my, and possibly the quartet's, reputation. We're up for a nice job as the quartet in residence at Lincoln Center. I think this might cost us our chance.

"I've been thinking and thinking and I might have a

solution. This is the only viable idea I've come up with."
Caitlin took a deep breath and continued. "I have a
proposition for you that involves a massive imposition. It's
the only solution I can dream up. I'm asking a lot of you,
but I don't know where else to turn. My whole future is at
stake."

"Wow, calm down," Mike said. "Let's talk about the
timing. How soon can you and Bruce marry? Could it be
before anyone can tell? If so, I don't think you have a
problem. The few pregnant women who plan to return to
work after having a baby almost always get a leave of
absence. In your case, you could wear loose-fitting clothes
and then leave a little early. Your leave might be a little
longer than some, but I don't see a problem."

"Nice idea, but it won't work," Caitlin responded.
"Hear me out. "If I take a leave for five months before the
baby is born, I would be gone for almost a year. The two
members of the quartet, other than Bruce, would likely
want to keep the second violinist they'd been practicing
with for that long. There are dozens of highly qualified
violinists who'd love to take my place—and keep it. As a
married woman, I could work at least three months longer
in my pregnancy. As a single one, no way. I believe the
group will take me back if I take the shorter leave. They
won't have the chance to grow too attached to the
substitute.

"That is why I am about to ask the world's biggest
favor of you. That's why I've got my courage up. I'm asking
if you will marry me just for a year. It would be a marriage
in name only. If you have a girlfriend back in Buffalo, she'd
never need to know. But you said you have nothing serious
going on anyway."

For a moment, Mike said nothing. Then he shook his head and said, "Wow. Your suggestion of a one-year marriage throws me for a loop. If we put our minds to it, I bet we can find another way. There's a lot to consider. For starters, a fake marriage is probably a sin. Then there is the fact that it would be totally disruptive to my life.

"I'm fond of the woman I've been dating back in Buffalo. I don't think it's serious, but I'm not sure. I can't imagine what she'd say if I said 'I'm getting married next weekend but can we still date?' Whatever her reaction, it wouldn't be pleasant—even if I told her it would be just for a year and done as a favor to an old friend. I need time to think about this. Are you sure that a nine- or ten-month leave would get you replaced?"

"Bruce and I feel it would be inevitable. There really are dozens of qualified violinists out there waiting tables and minding children while they wait for their big chance. Am I one hundred percent sure I'd be dumped? Of course not. However, the odds are not in my favor and it seems likely. Mike, I've thought and thought. No alternative comes to mind. I have nowhere else to turn. You're the big brother I never had. However, I must say that under these circumstances, I'm glad you're not really a relative.

"As I said, ours would be a marriage in name only. I'll be away most of the time. You wouldn't be supporting me, but you'd be saving the career I've worked so hard for. I've always counted on you when I had a real problem. You're the one who covered up for me when I hit the baseball through Mrs. McGarry's window."

"Well, this is certainly a different kind of cover-up," Mike said, slowly recovering his balance. "We're both good Catholics. A sham marriage is probably wrong in so many ways. We certainly couldn't be married in the church, but wrecking the career you've worked so hard for makes no sense either. I need a few days to think about this. For one thing, where would we live? I'm living with my folks now until I get a little money saved. Turns out, living in New York is a lot more expensive than living in Buffalo."

"You've always been like a little sister to me. I feel closer to you than to either of my older brothers. But there are a lot of things we'd have to work through. Give me a little time to think about this.

"In the meantime, why don't you find out what nearby states let people marry on short notice. We'd have to find a way to explain an elopement to our parents and why we didn't want to move in with them until we got on firmer financial ground."

Mike did not sleep well that night. As he tossed and turned, he tried to come up with a less disruptive plan. He failed. The next morning, he asked Caitlin to join him for breakfast. Over eggs, which he could barely eat, he reluctantly agreed to her scheme. Later that afternoon, they told Caitlin's father about their plans to elope.

Taken aback, Caitlin's father said, "You two getting married is great news. It's what we've always hoped for. But, why the elopement? We'd like nothing better than to give you a church wedding and a nice reception. That would mean a lot to your mother and to me."

"There is a little problem," Mike said quietly. "We've been pretty careful all our lives, but the night of my pal Pat's wedding, those of us in the bridal party had been provided with hotel rooms. They strongly, and rightly so, suspected we would drink too much to drive home safely. One thing led to another and well, your daughter is pregnant. She just found out for sure this week. We want to marry quietly and quickly so later no one knows the exact date. I know an elopement isn't what you two wished for us, but a speedy wedding seems the best idea."

After a minute, Caitlin's shocked father slowly said, "Well, I understand, but I will tell you what. We will have a party for you anyway, saying we just found out about your elopement. We will tell everyone that you did it this way because you did not want all the fuss of a big church wedding. That will help us all save face. However, I would still like you to be married again in a family-only ceremony in our church."

Mike gulped, thought fast and said, "Thank you for understanding and for the generous offer of the celebration. Still, let's put both the party and the wedding mass on hold—just for now."

At this point, Caitlin spoke up. "Dad, because of the pregnancy, we don't want *any* fuss or to give anyone the opportunity to ask us about the elopement date."

Caitlin's father nodded and agreed there would be no celebration.

Mike realized that he had better tell his friends at the *Buffalo Gazette* right away. He knew he should tell Nina first and he knew it wouldn't be pleasant. It would take courage, which he didn't seem to feel at the moment. Instead, he called Ralph first, his closest friend in the darkroom. When Ralph picked up the phone, Mike said, "I am calling to tell you that I am getting married in a few days. It will be at City Hall and just immediate family.

"I wanted you to know first. Please don't tell anyone, I want to keep this between us until I can tell Nina. I can't reach her now, but I will call her tonight." This of course was a lie.

"Who is this girl? What's she like? When did you meet her?" Ralph asked.

"I met her when I was six," Mike said with a grin. "That's when my family moved in next door to hers."

"Wow. What's she like?"

"Smart, pretty and an exceptionally talented musician," Mike answered. "You don't find many like her. You have to catch them when you can. She's in a string quartet that's about to leave on a month-long tour. I want to tie the knot before they hit the road."

"Wow again, and congratulations," Ralph stammered.

Within an hour of that call, everyone in the editorial department had heard the news, including Nina. When Mike finally reached her that evening, she said, "I heard the news in the office today. You're a pretty fast worker. Lots of luck."

Then she hung up. Her phone rang twice more and again early the next morning, but she didn't answer it. She feigned indifference when her friends from the Saturday Worth evenings asked her about it the next day.

That one phone call was the last time they spoke for eight years.

Chapter 8
KEVIN
1952

There was no way Mike and Caitlin could live with either set of parents and still have separate bedrooms. They did need to be near Caitlin's parents, who were going to mind the baby when the musicians were on tour. On the third apartment visit, they found not the ideal apartment, but one that would meet their needs for a moderately priced, two-bedroom unit in a safe neighborhood they could afford. To both sets of parents, they explained that they needed the two bedrooms for *Buffalo Gazette* friends who had quickly indicated that they planned to stay with the couple to save money on their New York City trips.

On a few lonely evenings, Mike tried to call Nina. As soon as she heard his "hello," she hung up the phone. Mike finally wrote her a letter. When it came, she tossed it in the garbage unread.

A month after the elopement, Caitlin's mother asked Mike why he didn't visit his bride on the weekends when the quartet was playing in the east. Mike thought she had a valid question. He called Caitlin about it. Although he had no plan to really visit, he thought he would go away some weekend and say he was visiting. The next time the quartet was playing in Philadelphia, he went off to a West Virginia golf clinic.

All went relatively well. Caitlin's married name was printed on the quartet's programs. She felt well enough to play through the first seven months of her pregnancy, although she was occasionally glad they had no morning concerts. She took off only two months before and three months after their son, Kevin, was born, not long enough for a substitute second violinist to settle in.

Back in New York, Mike was expected to pick up the baby each Sunday from Caitlin's parents' house. He couldn't have been less interested. He hadn't thought about this part of the deal. The new grandparents were infuriated at his attitude toward what they believed was his son.

As the months went by and baby Kevin developed a personality, he started to win Mike over. The two of them became regular Sunday morning visitors to the Central Park Zoo.

Bruce and Caitlin picked up the baby when they were in the New York area. Therefore, they were disappointed that Kevin's first word was directed toward Mike as "Daddy."

Bruce's divorce finally came through. Mike, Caitlin and Bruce discussed plans for coming clean. They started the annulment proceedings before they told their parents. When they did, all but Caitlin's dad exploded. He stayed calm and tried to calm the others. Later, he spoke to Mike.

"You're not Kevin's father, are you? I've suspected that from the beginning. The whole marriage was a way for you to protect Caitlin's reputation. I would guess the father is that Bruce who comes around often with Caitlin. Why didn't they just marry each other in the first place?" he asked.

"He was married at the time, although he and his wife had been separated for quite a while. The wife, now the ex-wife, lives in California. His divorce didn't come through before Caitlin's pregnancy began to show. She was afraid that not only *her* reputation but also the reputation of the *whole* quartet was at stake."

"You did a really great thing, Mike. Can I tell my wife and your parents?"

"I guess you can tell them," Mike answered, "But none of you can tell anyone else. Otherwise the whole marriage and all of its challenges will have been pointless.

Chapter 9
BETTY
1949

Betty Roeder was always a beauty with large blue eyes and blonde hair. She'd drawn admiring looks since the first time her mother put her in the carriage and took her for a walk in their Riverside neighborhood on the west side of Buffalo. Her years in elementary school showed that she was as bright as she was beautiful. By the time she got to Riverside High School, there were plenty of first dates but it soon became known that she was a "cold fish." Few of the first dates were followed up.

Betty's dad had been an independent house painter. During the depths of the Depression, he had found similar work with a large construction firm but with less income. Nonetheless, a hot meal was on the family dinner table each night. Unlike some of her friends, Betty never had to take catsup sandwiches to school. There was, however, no thought of college.

After high school graduation, she took the full-year course at the North Park Business School while working nights and weekends at Cooper's Market. First, she bagged groceries for the cashiers. When they realized how quick she was mathematically, mentally checking the cashiers' results, she became the store's youngest cashier.

Two days before her business school graduation, the head cashier approached thirty-six-year-old John Cooper to ask whether a small group could use the staff meeting room for a little party for Betty right after the store closed.

"We'll buy a cake," she volunteered. "We won't take long."

"I think we can afford to give you the cake," John, the store's owner said. Then, thinking about the pretty blonde, he added, "I'll come too."

The evening of the party, the head cashier made a one-minute speech praising Betty, mentioning how, with her mathematical mind, when still bagging groceries, she had caught another cashier (one no one liked) adding extra charges to the register receipts of aged or confused shoppers, then pocketing the difference. That cashier was fired immediately, and Betty was soon promoted.

During the graduation party, John Cooper decided that someone as bright as Betty, and who looked like Betty, should be doing bookkeeping in the company's main office—his office.

Betty was thrilled with her promotion. She was even happier a month later, when, one night after working late, John invited her to dinner. Soon the dinners became regular happenings. After several months, John invited her back to his apartment after dinner, stressing that his invitation was totally optional. He didn't want to lose that bookkeeper. He didn't need to worry. Betty hastily accepted the offer. Dinner and all that followed became a frequent event.

Then, late in 1949, nineteen-year-old Betty had an idea. John was single and he was obviously interested in her. She guessed that marriage was not on his radar. However, if she became pregnant, she presumed that would change. A few months later, when she was pretty sure that she was expecting, she asked John what he thought about children.

"I don't like kids. They're noisy and disturbing. I never want to have any," he announced. At that moment, Betty realized she had guessed wrong. She had no idea what to do. She wasn't particularly religious, but she would never consider an abortion. Still, she knew she had to hide the pregnancy from John, fearing he would leave her on hearing that news, given that he never wanted kids.

That night, she bravely told her mother the whole story.

"I'll think of something. Give me until tomorrow," her mother said quietly.

By the next evening, her mother had a plan.

"First of all," Mrs. Roeder said, "we've got time on our side. You work with ink. Ink can be messy. Long before you begin to show, start wearing a smock to work. Secondly, as you know, Aunt Sally was one of your favorite people before she married and moved to Minneapolis. Paul, her salesman husband, is on the road most weekdays. She's ten years younger than I am and has a ten-month-old baby and a three-year-old daughter. We'll tell her your problem. I bet she will be thrilled to have a live-in helper for a few months. The story we'll tell friends is that Sally is pregnant and has to stay off her feet. We'll add that she asked me, and I'm asking you to take a leave from your job and stay there to watch three-year-old Norma. Actually, you will be a tremendous help to her. I'm sure she'll be delighted to have you there. We'll say she needs day-to-day help. That will give you time to be in Minneapolis. When your baby is born, you'll put it up for adoption and come back home."

Listening to her mother, Betty felt a great weight lifted.

She followed the plan. The trusting John approved her leave and never doubted her reasons for the Minneapolis sojourn.

Chapter 10
THE BABY

Betty's baby was born three weeks early and was required to stay in the Minneapolis hospital for two extra weeks. The pediatrician told Betty she would have to bring the tiny girl in weekly for another two weeks so they could check on her.

"My mom in Buffalo is an obstetric nurse," Betty lied when they told her about the two extra weeks.

"If I take the baby to Buffalo, my mother will be there to watch her. I can also have her checked by a pediatrician there."

The doctor, who had noticed Betty's disinterest in the baby, thought this was a good idea. After a little research, he gave Betty the names of two pediatricians who worked out of what was then called Buffalo's Children's Hospital.

When Betty got back to Buffalo, Mrs. Roeder agreed to watch the infant for a few weeks until arrangements for adoption could be completed. Betty kept putting off her visit to the social worker to start the adoption process more out of inertia than any love she had developed for the infant. She clearly had little interest in the newborn and happily went back to work at the market in a few weeks.

"I missed you. The business missed you, but I missed you more," John said on the Monday morning she walked into the office. "I've given this a lot of thought while you were gone. I want to marry you. I'm nineteen years older than you, but I don't think that should matter between people who love each other. We will both be winners. You'll be my wife, and I'll make you vice president of the business. I already know that you have better ideas for it than I do."

Betty was not in love with John. She wasn't sure that she'd ever fall head over heels in love with anyone. She did like John. Moreover, she was totally in love with her role in the business. It took her less than a minute to almost shout, "Yes! What a wonderful welcome back!" With that, John exclaimed "Hallelujah!" and embraced her. Wasting no time, he added, "Could I come to your house tonight right after work and talk to your parents?"

Betty knew this was a terrible idea. The baby usually cried at dinnertime. She had read somewhere that the crying wasn't surprising, because that's the time expectant mothers are busy and under stress in the kitchen. Without checking her idea or consulting with anyone including her mother, Betty decided that if John was coming over near dinnertime, she would find some product she was sure must be on the market to help put a screaming infant to sleep.

Betty lied to John and said, "Oh tonight is my parent's bridge night. How about next Monday?" John checked his calendar and agreed to the new date.

When Monday arrived, Betty planned to stop at the drugstore to get the baby's sleep aid. She also wanted to buy a new dress. While on her lunch break, she got so involved with buying a dress for the occasion that she forgot the other stop. She remembered that evening just as she was getting dressed. In a panic, she looked in the medicine cabinet where, of course, there was nothing for a baby. The only thing that might work, she thought, was the cough medicine with codeine that her dad had used the winter before. She put some in the bottle of formula. Then, to be sure, she added a little more. She imagined it would make the infant sleep soundly that night. By the next day, the baby would be back on schedule.

Once the formula was altered, Betty went back to getting ready. There was barely enough time. Her future was at stake. After she fed the altered formula to the baby and burped her, Betty hurriedly put on the new print dress she had purchased on her lunch hour that day. When she put her hand in the pocket of the dress, she discovered a tiny bit of extra cloth resting on the seam. She pulled it out and thought she threw it in the bedroom waste basket. Actually, it stuck to her finger and then fell onto the side of the baby's diaper. In her haste, she didn't notice.

When John arrived, he took one look at her, smiled broadly and exclaimed:

"Whoa. You look great in that dress. Betty, you are truly beautiful! I want you to have a professional picture taken to commemorate this special evening and I want you to have your picture taken in that lovely dress.

"When we opened the newest store last year, a nice young photographer from the *Gazette* took pictures. He gave me his card saying he did portrait work on the side. I'll find his card and you can call him tomorrow."

At that point, Betty's parents entered the room. John got down to business and formally asked Mr. Roeder for his daughter's hand. Her father quickly gave his approval.

Chapter 11
THE LONG SLEEP

Much to the family's relief, the baby slept through the dinner hour and was quiet for the rest of the night. With all the excitement of the day, the whole family slept soundly that night.

It wasn't until Betty went to wake the baby the next morning that she realized the baby hadn't moved. She picked the infant up. Nothing. She gently shook the child. The baby didn't move or open her eyes. "Mom! Dad!" she screamed. Both came running. "I can't wake the baby!"

"What did you use to put her to sleep?" Mrs. Roeder asked, white-faced as she took the rigid infant from her daughter's arms.

"I just spooned a little of dad's old cough medicine into her bottle."

"Oh, my God! Oh my God! Oh my God! I think you've killed the child," Mrs. Roeder shrieked as she too was unable to wake the infant. Then she stood there silently and the tears formed. She kept standing there and shaking her head. Then, she did what she always did when facing a problem. She steadied herself and asked her husband for advice.

"Shall we call the police? Shall we call Father Garrity?" he offered. Mrs. Roeder shook her head.

"I have to think," she muttered. "Give me a little time. Betty accidentally poisoned the baby," Mrs. Roeder cried.

"I have to figure out what we should do."

"You're probably overreacting. The baby may just be a sound sleeper," Mr. Roeder said as he grabbed the still infant from his wife's arms. The baby did not move. He shook her again, this time with more effort. The baby still didn't stir. For a full two minutes, they all stood there silently, staring at each other.

Betty broke the silence with a loud moan. "It was an accident! It was an accident. What will I do? My life is ruined!" Betty wailed and began to sob hysterically.

Something in Betty's crying snapped Mrs. Roeder out of her tailspin. She had a flash of clarity. "Wait," she said, turning to Mr. Roeder. "No one around here knows that this baby exists. There's no birth record in the State of New York. You haven't been to the adoption agency yet to fill out the papers. The baby is clearly dead. We can't bring it back, but we can save Betty's future. We have to get rid of the baby somewhere where no one will be able to tie it to us. Let's wrap it up and take it way out into woods, far from here."

"You can't do that. It would be a sin and a crime," Mr. Roeder said sternly.

"We can't throw away our daughter's future," his wife argued. "She might even be arrested for murder. We have to do something. Let's think for a few more minutes."

After what felt like a week but was really five minutes with Betty still moaning, Mrs. Roeder spoke again. Turning to her husband, she said, "Go to Woolworths after work. Buy a covered basket where we can put the body. Wear gloves when you pick it up so there are no fingerprints. Then, drive somewhere where there are woods. Go in a mile or so from the road and hide the basket. It's the only thing I can think of."

Mr. Roeder numbly decided to follow his wife's plan. Betty just sat there weeping.

Halloween had been only three weeks earlier. Large plastic pumpkins at Woolworth's were marked down. Picnic baskets were nowhere to be found. Betty's dad bought an extra-large plastic pumpkin that came with a lid.

In the years that followed, he felt uncomfortable every time he was near a policeman, even if it was just the man on the next stool at his favorite bar. He had nightmares for a few months, but when no one came forward to ring his doorbell and the newspapers had long lost interest in the story of the infant found in the woods, he relaxed a little. But Mr. Roeder never forgot what he and his family had done. He was always uncomfortable in church and never again went to confession.

Chapter 12
ANDY
1953

Nina rarely ate in the *Gazette* lunchroom. She either brought her sandwich or went across the street from the paper with Elaine, the theater reporter. But one rainy, sandwich-less day, she wandered into the decidedly mediocre ground floor lunch room at the *Gazette*, bought some soup, saw the new reporter, Andy Conway, and sat down across from him.

"Tell me about those cowboy boots you're always wearing," she said. "They tell me you came here from Syracuse. That's not cattle country."

"I did come here from Syracuse, but I was raised in North Dakota. My dad teaches literature at North Dakota State. During the war, I was in the South Pacific during rainy season. My boots were always soggy. I promised myself that if I ever I got home, I'd buy a first-class pair of cowboy boots and wear them every day. They remind me of home."

"I hope you don't mind my curiosity," Nina said. "I hear you're covering art and architecture." "I majored in art history at North Dakota. Then, I came east for journalism at Syracuse. I got a part-time job at the Post Standard, covering high school sports while I was in grad school. I was able to get a general assignment job there after I graduated.

"I know who you are," he added. "I asked the guy at the next desk who the cute girl was. He gave me your name and said you were single. Would you be willing to give me your phone number? I've got to dash now. I'm interviewing a young artist who lives on Potomac Avenue. He told me that's just off Elmwood. Where's Elmwood?"

Although she wasn't exactly sure why, Nina was charmed in that first short conversation and gave him directions and her phone number.

That evening, he called. "A road company of 'Brigadoon' is coming to the Erlanger Theater this weekend. Would you like to go with me Friday or Saturday night?"

"What a nice invitation, sure. Saturday's better. I don't work Sundays. Do you?"

"No. Saturday is better for me too. I just wanted to give you a choice."

Andy picked her up at home that Saturday evening, meeting her mother who was standing in the living room. Looking around, Andy spotted the Hanukah menorah in the open bookcase.

"Are you Jewish?" he asked, not that the name Silver hadn't indicated that in the first place. "I'm told our family name was Cohen before my dad moved to North Dakota and changed it."

With that remark, he won over Mrs. Silver. Sometimes in later years, she wondered whether he'd been telling the truth, but she had decided to take him at his word.

That first theater date led to many more. They spent most weekends together. In late February, Andy took Nina on a weekend ski trip to Killington, Vermont, with a couple of their good friends.

She'd fallen in love again, and once more with a good man. The next year, when he asked her to marry him, she found herself saying "yes" very quickly.

Three days after they told Nina's parents about their plans to marry, Mrs. Silver handed Nina a sheet of paper before the couple left to go to dinner.

"I worked late last night making a list of one hundred fifty-four friends and relatives to invite to your wedding. You can add your own friends too. Don't worry about the cost. Your dad and I expect to pay. It's what the bride's family does."

Andy went pale as a ghost. Grabbing Nina's arm, he hurried her out the door, announcing: "We've got to go or we'll be late for our reservation."

As soon as they were in his car, a white-faced Andy, who hated to be the center of attention, stated, "I want to marry you more than anything else in the world, but not in front of two hundred people. What would you think about eloping? Your mother scared the wits out of me."

"I hadn't thought about it before, but I bet we could move our vacations to the first or second week in December. Winter Park, Colorado, would be the perfect place for a wedding. We can tell your folks we're going on a ski week and that we will talk wedding plans when we come back. I know you can get married on the Winter Park slopes. I once saw a wedding there. That seems pretty romantic to me, although it will probably be more than a little brisk. I'm sure we would have to make arrangements ahead of time. One of my college friends got married in Aspen. I'll call him and ask how he went about it."

Nina was quiet for a moment. "When I was a little girl playing with paper dolls, I would make wedding dresses for them from the white ceiling-paper pages in old wallpaper sample books I'd been given. I suppose that was then. This is now," she said with a faraway look.

After a moment, she smiled and said, "You are right. I don't want to spend the next six months worrying about what kind of flowers to carry and what design I want on the icing of a wedding cake. I certainly don't want to spend time or money looking for a long white wedding dress that I will never wear again. I think a warm ski jacket would make the perfect wedding attire. Making out lists of who to invite and who to leave out would also drive me crazy.

"Now that you have suggested it, I love the idea of eloping. You are right: we can each request earlier vacation time. People want time off for the holidays. The paper will not be short on staff three weeks earlier. Yes, I'm for eloping," Nina repeated.

They made no secret of their engagement and both applied for vacation time the first week in December. Andy made the reservations for Winter Park. That is where he had learned to ski as a boy and where he and his college buddies spent spring break during their undergraduate years.

"It's beautiful there. It won't be crowded two or three weeks before the Christmas holidays," he said. "The resort is on the right side of the mountains for early season snowfall. Winter Park gets snow earlier than some places."

Two weeks before their scheduled vacation, Managing Editor Jack Clark called Nina in for a talk. It was the first time she had spoken with him since he hired her.

"Congratulations. I hear through the grapevine that you and Andy Conway are getting married. I also hear that you are planning to return to work after your marriage. It seems to me that women don't do that, except in cases of poverty, but in any case, we have a policy at the paper. Husband and wife can't both work here. It would look like nepotism."

At that time, Buffalo had two daily papers, the *Evening Gazette* and the morning paper, *The Courier Express*.

"Wouldn't it be worse if I went to work at the *Courier* while Andy was working here?" Nina asked.

"Interesting. Given that choice, I will have to give the matter some thought," Clark answered.

A few days later, Nina got a note from Clark. "You can stay. We just won't change your byline to Conway. We'll move your desk far from Andy's. You're both good reporters. I'd hate to lose you. How about we give you a chance? However, because I don't want you two sitting near each other, we'll move you upstairs with the radio and TV reporters."

Nina wasn't delighted about where she was to sit. She would miss the commotion of the newsroom, but she was very happy to be able to keep her job.

The wedding in Winter Park that December went just as they had hoped. It was a crisp, sunny day that they both would always remember.

When they returned from their honeymoon, Nina's mother lost no time telling them how furious she was.

"Well," she said, "we'll have to have a party for you anyway. We can't get a mob in this house, so we will have it in the Park Lane. They have lovely banquet rooms. I don't want to hear any arguments."

"I know you're not wild about big parties, Andy," Nina said later, "but it will only be a couple of hours. My mom can have half the guests come at one hour and the other half, two hours later. They'll all be chatting with each other and won't be paying much attention to us except for a quick handshake. My mother's friends won't stay too long at a cocktail party where they have to stand up the whole time. We will always have our memories of our private, slope-side wedding without crowds or chaos."

Chapter 13
SETTLING IN

Nina and Andy had given little prior time to apartment hunting. Andy's studio apartment was too small a space in which to begin a marriage. Neither of them thought for a minute about moving in with her parents, even for a short time.

"I'd like to buy a house soon," Andy said," but I want to take enough time to make sure we make a smart choice. Let's rent a furnished apartment downtown in a building that caters to people whose work brings them here for just a short while."

Nina agreed and that is what they did. Seven months later, they found a five-year-old, one-story house in the town of Clarence, a thirty-five-minute drive to the *Gazette*. It had a big kitchen, two baths, a large family room and three bedrooms.

"We both want kids, and I don't want to wait too long to have them. Buying a house now will give us a chance to get settled in it before that happens," Andy said. Nina agreed.

Most of Nina's friends, if they worked after marriage, quit when they started a family. Nina had no intention of following their example.

"I know that many people feel that if a kid comes home from school and isn't greeted by his mother and the smell of home baking, he'll be deprived. I don't agree," she told almost everyone she knew.

Two years later, she held true to her word when she realized that her first child was on the way. When she informed the managing editor that she would like two months off before the baby came and four after, he told her, "You're very lucky. This paper has a maternity leave policy that pre-dates my arrival here. You leave before your pregnancy shows and come back in as few weeks after the birth as possible. Four months off before and two months after. You will get your old job back or a similar one. Of course, we won't pay you when you are not here."

Nina had never heard of paid maternity leave so that part didn't bother her. The plan wasn't exactly what she had hoped for, but Nina was delighted that she could return to the *Gazette*.

When her friends asked why she went back to work when her son Jonathan was just two months old, she repeated what she'd said before:

"If I'd married a doctor like my dad or a lawyer, I might have had to quit my job lest people think my husband wasn't doing very well and was a second-rate practitioner. With a salaried newspaperman, it doesn't seem to matter. To tell the truth, I really like my job. I missed it when I was on leave. I enjoy going to work each day and Jonathan is pure joy to me when I get home. If I had waited a few more months to return to work, Jonathan would have developed his cute personality and it would have been so much harder to leave him."

Nina found a sitter who would come to work by eight every morning and stay until after five, when at least one of them returned home. Between taxes and the sitter's salary, Nina didn't clear much money, but she was happy.

She and the baby had fun together when she came home each evening.

Neither Mike O'Neill nor the unsolved murder entered her thoughts much during the busy years that followed.

BOOK TWO

Chapter 14
1960

In her black pinstripe skirt suit, Nina felt pretty good about herself as she stepped into the revolving door of New York City's Plaza Hotel that late June afternoon. She was on her way to cover a showing of women's fall and winter fashions even though the thermometer she had passed on her lunch walk read 83 degrees.

The door began to turn before she even pushed it. She looked through the glass and was startled to see Mike O'Neill. She called out. He turned, exiting the door on the street side. She exited on the hotel side. Both laughed. Second time around she stayed in the lobby. He came back in, a heavy camera bag hanging from his shoulder. There was time for an overly long hug and a kiss before someone wanting to enter the hotel complained that they were blocking the doorway.

Almost in unison, they both asked, "What are you doing here?"

"I write features now. That includes covering the fall and winter fashion shows in New York," said Nina. "I can't believe I ran into you in this massive city."

"It's not as unusual as you think in midtown. We New Yorkers walk. In Buffalo, you drive everywhere." He flashed the old familiar smile. At that moment, she realized that, although she very much loved her husband, she had never really stopped caring for Mike.

"I'm glad to hear you're not still queen of the obituary page," Mike said. "I'm here because I just took a fashion shot for Bill Blass for the September *Charm* magazine. I took one a few weeks ago," he said, "but, then Blass had a new idea. He wanted one model having her dress fastened and two more having their hair combed in the photo. He was paying the models today anyway, so that is why I did the re-shoot here." Mike laughed. "I am sure that is much more detail than you wanted."

He continued: "Do you have to go now, or can we go somewhere and talk? I'd love to know what you're up to. It's been a long time and yet the memories are still strong and always make me smile."

Nina grinned and responded, "I have enough notes on the big-name designers from this morning. I can skip the afternoon showings and still have enough to write about. I'd love to hear about your photography business and your married life."

"The photography business is going really well. I have enough business now to freelance. I do fashion shoots and portraits. I must admit, I'm making a good living. I love what I do. On the home front, I am no longer married. That marriage lasted just a year, but long enough for the arrival of Kevin. He's now seven. He lives with me during the school year and a little of the summer. Caitlin, his mother, plays in a string quartet that is in residence from late June through much of August at the Aspen Music School. He goes with her to Colorado when she's in residence there. Kevin left just a few days ago and already I am missing him."

Mike purposely never mentioned or even thought to mention that he wasn't really Kevin's father. He rarely mentioned that to anyone but Kevin, who was always told, before he headed west, that he was going to visit his "real parents," although as a three-, four- and five-year-old, he had no idea what that meant.

One night, in his nursery school years, Kevin had abruptly asked at dinner, "My friend Timmy has two mothers and two fathers. Why do I have two fathers but only one mother?"

Without going into details, Mike had said, "It must be because Timmy's mother and father both married twice. I never married a second time."

"You could marry my nursery schoolteacher. She's pretty and nice."

"Well, yes, but since I don't know her, I don't think that's a good idea." Mike chuckled and then changed the subject. When the question of parenthood was brought up again years later, Mike simply explained that he and Caitlin couldn't stay married because she travelled so frequently. But at this moment, Mike could see no reason to go into any of those details with Nina. Instead, he changed the subject.

"What about you?" he asked Nina.

"I'm married to a wonderful man named Andy Conway. He came to the paper shortly after you left. We have a three-year-old son, Jonathan."

"Let's stop blocking traffic here. A quiet bar in the Hilton is just a few blocks away. I'd love to see pictures of Jonathan and show you some of Kevin. I don't want to have a drink here in case Blass spots me and decides to take his advertising picture over, yet another different way."

"That works for me since that is my hotel this week.

Let's go."

With that, they walked out the door and strolled the three blocks to the Hilton bar. Both realized that their hearts were beating faster than normal, and it wasn't because of the walk. Neither said anything about it, but each realized that first love doesn't always fade away. They jabbered away about their sons and, at first, made no mention of their previous relationship.

Finally, Nina, bold as usual, asked, "How come you never remarried?"

"Maybe because you were a tough act to follow," Mike said, looking straight into her eyes and grabbing her hand.

Nina took a quick breath. "I love my husband. He is a great guy. But I've never forgotten my time with you. I think people can hold more than one person in their hearts."

Mike ignored the comment and continued, "You say you're married to a guy named Conway. That's not a Jewish name. What did your mother have to say about your marriage?"

"Ah," Nina said, "you remember that twist. Andy says his family's name was Cohen a generation back. He hasn't practiced any religion for years. His dad teaches literature at the University of North Dakota. That's where he grew up. I'd guess there's not a big Jewish community in Grand Forks.

Nina went on, "We joined a temple last year and have been twice. Andy had no objection and it made my mother's day. She gave him a chance and found she liked him. He is a very charming man."

"I guess I'm not as devout as I should be either. Kevin goes to a private Catholic school, but when he's with me, we usually don't make it to Mass. It may be different when he's with Caitlin. I've never asked."

To again change the subject, he asked her if the pumpkin shell murder had ever been solved.

"No," Nina answered, "but I think about it from time to time. It still bugs me after all these years. Everyone just let it drop. I hope I can help solve it someday. No one but me seems to care anymore."

After the waitress came by for the second time to ask if she could refill their glasses and after they shook their heads "no" for the second time, Mike stood up, put his hand over Nina's and got ready to leave. He was shocked when Nina spoke her mind.

"If you walk out that door, I'll probably never see you again. I am a happily married woman, but a part of me is still taken with you." Nina leaned in and looked straight into Mike's eyes. " Do you really have to go? I never thought 'what if?' until the revolving door. Way back when, I was in love with you. Could we for one evening bring back the old magic? You know me well enough to know, I always speak my mind. If you say 'forget about it,' I will try. I hope I'm not shocking you, although I suppose I am. Actually, I am rather shocking myself. Some people say that there's no such thing as a coincidence. Maybe fate brought us together to do more than talk about our sons," Nina added.

Quietly, Mike said, "You're married, and I have Catholic school guilt. Nonetheless, that's the best offer I've had in a very long time. However, I don't think the 'best offer' is always a good idea. It is an idea that certainly shouldn't come from a woman who says she's happily married. Were you drinking your lunch before we met in the revolving door?"

"My lunch was a chicken sandwich at Schraft's and a cup of coffee, thank you very much. It's just that when you stood up to leave just now, I realized this could be it for us and our paths might never cross again. The words just tumbled out. An afternoon that refreshes old memories would just be a shot at closure," Nina persisted.

Then another thought ran through her head. She and Andy had been trying unsuccessfully to have another child for the past year. She had heard about childless couples who suddenly were able to conceive after they adopted one and the pressure was off. Maybe a tiny bit of adultery would do the trick. After all, the two men had similar coloring and both were just shy of six feet. If she never knew which man was her second child's father, it wouldn't matter. She would know it was someone she had loved and someone who, by all standards, was a good man.

Mike still hesitated. "Are you sure about this?" he asked hearing from both the angel and the devil on his shoulder.

She nodded.

The devil won. He thought, "Why not?"

"Tell me your room number. I'll make a drugstore stop and meet you there."

"No need," Nina lied. "I have a protective implant that's always in place. It's much more convenient than the old way."

Maybe because it was illicit. Maybe because the first love had never died. Whatever the reason, the sex left them both feeling on top of the world.

"I guess I should be honored. You've probably slept with some of America's most beautiful models," Nina said as they were getting ready to leave the hotel room.

"First of all, sleeping with a vacuum-brained, seventeen-year-old clothes hanger would not only be boring but also illegal," Mike answered. "Sure, I've bedded some of the older models. But they don't see me as a person, just as someone who might help them keep working in what is a very young person's business."

"Well, to me you're one sexy person. I'm here once a year," Nina announced, her head still spinning. "This was too great to be a one-afternoon stand. If you're still unattached next year, I'm in favor of an annual reunion. I love my husband, but I think our little get-together was a dash of pepper in the good stew of our lives."

"Whoa there, girl! I don't know. Didn't you say this was about closure? I'll deal with the moral issue later. Then again, you are one of the best things that ever happened to me. That said, and because I'm no fool, until I think better of it, you're on. I'll put down 'late June,' with a big question mark when I get my new calendar. Fantastic as this afternoon has been, I'm not at all sure an annual replay is a good or a moral thing. But I have to agree the magic has lasted."

Then he headed for the door. Turning, he said, much against his better judgment, "My business is in the Manhattan yellow pages under my own name. Call me when you're next in New York."

Chapter 15
JENNIFER
1961

Nina was back home later the next night and made sure to cozy up to Andy.

Eight weeks later, she learned she was pregnant. She didn't know and never wanted to know which man was the father. She chose to believe it was Andy. It most likely was, she told herself.

The proud new parents named the baby Jennifer. With her first smile, she won the lifelong adoration of Nina, Andy and Jonathan, who by then was always referred to as Jon. As she had done with Jon, Nina again returned to work when the new baby was two months old.

"Repeating myself from the first time around, if I wait too long, the kid will be too cute to leave, so I am going back to work now," she told friends, who again clearly disapproved of her returning to work so soon.

The following June, in New York again, after some debate with herself, she called Mike. The fall fashion showings began early on a Monday morning, but she'd flown to Newark the Friday before for a forty-eight-hour showing of menswear in Spring Lake on the New Jersey shore. After the Sunday morning showings, the reporters were bussed into Manhattan to be ready for the women's wear shows at The Plaza Hotel early the next morning.

She had phoned Mike a few weeks ahead. He had given

her the address of the east-side brownstone that was his now his home and studio.

After arriving in Manhattan, she called home before heading to Mike's place.

Andy had taken both Jon and tiny Jennifer to the Buffalo Zoo that afternoon and announced that a good time was had by all.

Nina hung up the phone, ran a comb through her hair and took a cab from the Plaza to East 38th between Second and Third Avenues.

The address Mike had given her was a four-story town house, easily spotted because, unlike every other house on the block, it had a bright kelly-green door. There was no big window as at the photographers' studios she'd seen at home. There was no large sign, just a small gold nameplate that read simply: "Michael O'Neill" and just below, the words "Portrait Photography."

Mike opened the door almost instantly and ushered Nina into his main-floor studio where he gave her a long, tight hug.

The reception room had a counter and two large photos on the wall. One was of a large family and the other of a bride descending the curved staircase at the left of the foyer. In the studio itself, walls and drapes were ivory-colored. A large, costly looking, three-piece, ivory couch drew Nina's attention.

"I believed that luxury would bring in luxury when I bought that couch. It has," Mike told Nina.

The many floodlights in the room, he explained, would not only brighten a gloomy day but could turn the walls to a soft blue, pink or green to contrast with a bride's white dress. A Miro print hung on one wall. A framed reprint of an impressionist French scene rested on the floor just below it. Nearby was a small walnut table.

"Some people like to have a homelike background in their photograph," Mike said. "As for the couch, when the three parts are together, it can accommodate a family group. If I separate one end, I can drape a model on it for an alluring perfume ad.

"In fact," he said with a glint in his eye, "I could drape you there, clothed or not, and take your picture."

"No thanks," Nina said quickly. "Our relationship calls for memories, not souvenirs."

Mike smiled. "I'll show you where I live. I bought this building last year. I rent out the third and fourth floors. I live on the second floor."

Nina smiled in surprise when she climbed up to the second floor and saw his apartment's living room. Unlike the studio below, his apartment furniture looked like it had come from the Salvation Army. However, it all went well together. The three white and one tangerine wall showed Mike's eye for color. The room had only a regular double bed and all the charm of a cheap hotel room.

Noticing her facial expression, Mike commented, "If you note the under-decorated look of this room, Kevin's room averages it out." With that, he opened the door to the second bedroom where almost every inch of wall space was covered with posters of soccer stars and sailboats.

Back in Mike's room, Nina said, "I thought that an eligible, single guy like you would have a king-size bed."

"When Kevin is away, if I bring someone here," he said with a mischievous grin, "I like to hold her close, like this," as he took Nina into his arms.

None of the electricity had been lost since the previous

June. They whiled away the afternoon and then went to dinner at a small bistro in the neighborhood.

"How long are you in New York?" he asked over coffee.

"I go home Tuesday evening," she said.

Figuring that two nights of mischief were no more cause for guilt than one, he kissed her on the cheek and asked, "Can you join me again tomorrow evening?"

The next June, they repeated their annual adventure. Nina knew then that she did indeed love two men simultaneously.

As Mike left her in the early morning of that Tuesday in June, he announced:

"These annual get-togethers have been great. I'll never forget them, but this has to be the last time. I'm getting married in a few months. It has to work this time. I'm going to be totally faithful. The sex will not be as good as it's been with you, but Marian will be there for breakfast and dinner, day after day. She's a social worker in Westchester, reads a lot, gets along beautifully with Kevin and is interesting and fun to be with. There are no fireworks, but I can live with that. She's good company and Kevin needs a woman in the house. So do I."

"I'm glad for you, but honestly, more than a little sorry for me," Nina said. As she left after the customary hug and kiss, she said sadly what she thought was their last goodbye. As she flew home, she cheered herself up with thoughts of her wonderful Clarence family.

Time flew. Nina returned home to her job and her family. Both Nina and Andy doted on the children. In time, weekday evenings were devoted to word or board games or to reading to the children. When they were still small, Andy assigned chores to them so they could learn from the start to be helpful. When Nina and Andy went out with friends, it was only on Saturday nights. The children, left with a young sitter, delighted in the rare TV dinners that were always supplemented by French pastries from a special bakery in town.

The couple had two weeks of paid vacations and, after ten years, three weeks. Thanks to the two salaries, the couple took a winter and a summer vacation each year. The summer vacation always included the children.

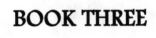

BOOK THREE

Chapter 16
ACCIDENT AT THE MARKET
1973

Shortly before Jonathan's sixteenth birthday, Nina asked him if he'd like a party—with six or eight of his friends for bowling and then back to the house for a cookout.

"I don't really care one way or the other about a party. What I'd really like would be if one of you could drive me to the Department of Motor Vehicles that day so I could get my learner's permit. Then, maybe the four of us could go out for steak."

Andy wasn't happy at the thought of Jonathon driving. "Your mother and I use our two cars for work. We usually go off in separate directions," he told Jon. He added, "Gasoline is expensive. Besides, you would rarely get to use one of our cars."

"Come on Dad—all I am asking is that I have the chance to learn the basics so I can do well in Driver's Ed at school next term. Besides, one or both of your cars sit around most Saturdays and Sundays. When you go out in the evening, you use only one car. I wouldn't be allowed to drive alone unless it was to a daytime job. But-I could get a job, quite likely at the Cooper's Market here in Clarence. Sam is moving to Cleveland with his mom. I bet I could get his job. Then I would have more spending money."

"I'll agree to the steak, but let me think about the

driving," Andy said.

He and Nina talked it over that evening. Nina suggested that a part-time job might be a good lesson in responsibility. Andy came around.

The following week, Andy took Jon to the Department of Motor Vehicles to get his learner's permit.

Shortly after, Jon did get a job on Saturday and Sunday afternoons at Cooper's Market. He bicycled to work at first, waiting six months before he took his driver's test. Andy had insisted that he had to complete his high school's summer safe-driver's training program before he could take his driver's test.

He was still cycling to work several months later, when on a busy Saturday afternoon, an eighty-seven-year-old man drove his car into the doorway of the market. He jarred the building so that a tall pyramid of canned tomatoes, set up just inside the front doors, collapsed. It knocked down six shoppers coming and going at that minute. Jon and the others at the cash registers stopped what they were doing and ran to help. Jon picked up an elderly woman who had fallen. It was less than five minutes after the accident when the manager ran from the back of the store to the front amid all the commotion.

He gathered the employees who were helping and quietly said:

"I've just talked to Mrs. Cooper at company headquarters. She wants you all to go back to your jobs immediately. Medical help and police will be here soon to take care of any one who is hurt. She wants to be sure that in this chaos, no one leaves the store with unpaid groceries."

The employees exchanged surprised glances but did as

they were ordered. Still, they were shaken.

The whole episode upset Jon so much, he discussed it with his parents at dinner that night.

"Shouldn't the first concern have been with the injured?" he asked. "There might have been some broken bones. I doubt anyone would have tried to steal a jar of jam or whatever, but it wouldn't have made a difference in the company's profits. Something is wrong with this management." He paused and added, "I don't think I want to work in a place with those values."

"I agree with what you say in faulting Mrs. Cooper's values." Andy said. "You can quit if you want. However, it won't have any effect on the Coopers. On the other hand, it will be hard for you to find another weekend job that close to home. Someday, if you have a full-time job in a small business, quitting to make a moral point will make a significant statement. Here it won't. Your mother and I will support you either way. You have to decide what to do."

Nina listened to the conversation, nodded and commented half to herself, "It's just proof that that woman is unfeeling and heartless." In front of Jon, she didn't add "and maybe a murderer," but it was what she thought.

Jon stayed at the job through the rest of high school. He did, however, get his mother to switch her shopping from Cooper's to Quality Markets, just a mile further from home. It didn't take much convincing.

Chapter 17
BETTY AS BOSS
1977

Betty and John Cooper were married for twenty-six years before his death. Although the only grand passion of Betty's life was her work at the markets, theirs was a pleasant marriage. She had made a promise to herself to be a good wife, to have dinner on the table each night after they got home and to make few demands.

Shortly after they married, when John was thinking of opening a new store on the city's busy Elmwood Avenue, she quietly suggested that in those post–World War II years, veterans and their young families were moving to the suburbs. They weren't walking to a neighborhood food market. They were driving to do their grocery shopping and not doing it daily. She convinced John. Their new store was built in the northern Buffalo suburb of Kenmore and had a huge parking lot. When they were planning the next store, a few years later, John sought his wife's opinion on its location. She suggested West Seneca, the suburb immediately south of the city.

As her responsibilities with the chain grew, Betty kept up on what the best in the business were doing and how they were expanding. She subscribed to *Progressive Grocer*, *Supermarket News* and *Grocery Headquarters* and read them all thoroughly. It was her suggestion for the store to open a deli counter and to sell sandwiches, made to order, as well as to provide in-store tables and chairs. She also suggested the store always have hot coffee for sale, as reasonably priced as possible.

When a few of John's friends retired and began twice-weekly golf games, he completed their foursome and came late to the store after eighteen holes. He regarded his marriage as the best thing that ever happened to him. Betty not only ran a comfortable home but also was a far better manager for a growing business than he would have been on his own. She saved much of her paycheck. With that money, she bought her parents one of the charming one-story houses going up in the Kenmore area. They were called "ranch" homes, though neither in house size nor acreage did they resemble what any westerner would call "a ranch." The grocery chain and John's golf game both thrived with this new arrangement.

Years later, after John died, Betty went ahead with plans for the largest store yet, even farther from the city. When she went to negotiate a new loan from the bank that Cooper's Markets had always used, she was flabbergasted to be turned down.

Later that same afternoon, when her banker was playing his regular 5:00 p.m. squash game at the Saturn Club, he remarked to his partner, "You'll never guess what happened today. A widow, the one from Cooper's Markets, who doesn't even have a college degree, tried to take out a million-dollar loan. She was startled when we said 'no.' I don't know what these uppity women are thinking these days."

Angry but undeterred, Betty tried a second bank. Then a third, this time with one that was expanding. The third time was the charm. The bankers checked Cooper's

Markets' financial history and told Betty they would grant the loan if she appointed a board of directors, made up of male community leaders with deep financial experience.

Betty explained that she had been running the markets for over 20 years, but the banker shook his head. "No board of directors, no men to guide you, no loan," he insisted. Betty reluctantly agreed to appoint a board and to select the directors from the list the bank gave her.

Chapter 18
CAUGHT IN THE ACT
1981

In 1981, Nina was named an editorial writer at the *Buffalo Gazette*, the first woman to ever hold that position. Shortly after her appointment, she was designated one of the five "Women of the Year" by *Western New York Business* magazine. Andy went with her to the annual awards luncheon.

Nina felt confident as she and Andy entered the Hotel Statler banquet room for the awards ceremony that May day. She wore a short-sleeve black dress with a bright, canary-yellow jacket.

A few weeks earlier she had read the list of the other honorees. Third on the alphabetical list of five was Betty Cooper. The photo in the paper showed a younger Betty in Mike's old photo where she wore the dress that matched the scrap of fabric found long ago with the body in the pumpkin. Because of that photo, Nina had always believed that Mrs. Cooper was the one responsible for the 1950 murder of that infant. The junior detective in her reawakened. She couldn't help but wonder whether this luncheon would provide an opportunity to put some facts around her long-time hunch.

Betty, a widow for years now, had long been running the market business. Under her leadership, the chain had grown from five grocery stores into a fourteen-market chain. The new stores were in midsized towns, beyond the suburbs that spread out from the city. Betty had guessed correctly that they would soon boom. The stores carried a bigger variety of items than had been available in the area before. Each gave employment to from three to four hundred local area residents. As the chain prospered, gossip said that Betty was a better businessperson than her husband had ever been. Upon his death, she became the president in name as well as in actuality.

Nina, the first of the nominees to arrive at the luncheon, discreetly moved the place cards at the honorees' table so that she could sit next to Betty Cooper.

Betty arrived at the luncheon alone. She looked beautiful in a navy silk jacket dress. Her very blonde hair and bright red lipstick were a little too much for Nina's preppy taste but she had to admit that Betty Cooper was a most attractive woman.

Once they sat down, there were brief opening comments, a speech from the mayor and a glass of wine for all at the speaker's table. Emboldened by the drink and taking advantage of the pause in the proceedings while lunch was served, Nina lost no time in talking with Betty. After a few general questions about the size of the chain, she asked her:

"You have such a large chain of markets. Do your children help you run the stores?"

"I have no children," Betty responded. "I had a wonderful husband, but he didn't want children."

Equally talkative after her glass of wine, Betty continued, "In fact, he often said he didn't even like them. In his opinion, they made too much noise and took up too much of one's time."

Nina's imagination went wild. It all tied together. Of course, she still had to prove her case. When they finished eating and Betty made a trip to the ladies' room, Nina saw her chance. She swiftly switched her clean spoon with Betty's used one. Then carefully, she put Betty's used spoon into her purse. She was going to solve that old murder case with the new DNA technology she had read about.

A few minutes later, during a pause in the program before the plaques were presented, Nina made her way off the dias and toward Andy's table. As she did, a uniformed hotel employee approached her.

"Excuse me, madam. Can I speak with you for a minute?" he asked. She gasped. "Did I get a call from the paper? Is something wrong?"

"No. Nothing like that," the guard explained in a very soft voice. Andy heard none of it.

"Excuse me," she said to Andy. "I'll be right back."

When they were out of earshot, the uniformed man said simply:

"Madam, the waiter saw you pocket your spoon. We can't allow that. You don't need a souvenir. You're going to get a plaque."

"The waiter was very observant," she said, hoping flattery would help in this awkward situation. "Let me explain." Somewhat flustered, she added, "Actually it's not my spoon. It's from the honoree sitting next to me. I am an investigative reporter and I think her DNA may help solve an old case."

"I've heard many excuses in my day. I have to admit yours is a new one. Just give me the spoon and we'll forget the whole thing."

"But I need it for the DNA."

"Sorry lady. I need it for inventory."

Nina thought for a moment. "Can I rub it clean with a paper napkin, give the spoon back to you and keep the napkin?"

"That's okay with me. You may have all the paper napkins that you like. Guess they really don't pay you that well at the paper."

Nina scowled, rubbed the spoon and carefully folded the paper napkin. She put it in the small black purse she was carrying and wondered, if she had worn a dull grey dress instead of a bright yellow jacket that day, whether her spoon thievery would have been noticed.

"What was that all about?" Andy asked when she got back to the table." Is everything okay?"

"Yes, fine. I'll explain in the car on the way home."

On the ride home, she told Andy the full story of her first and only murder assignment. How years ago, she had seen the portrait of the soon-to-be Mrs. Cooper wearing a dress made of fabric that matched the bit of cloth caught at the edge of the dead baby's diaper. She did not mention where she had seen the portrait.

"That was more than thirty years ago," Andy said, laughing. "Leave it alone. If the baby's murderer was Mrs. Cooper, and I think your idea is probably crazy, no one is going to do anything about it. Betty Cooper has done more than almost anyone in this city to create jobs in this area. She strikes me as a very smart woman. There is no way anyone will exhume that baby's body, even if they knew where to look for it. This isn't some television show. Now let's go home and celebrate your most impressive accomplishments and usually rational ideas."

Nina paid no attention to his advice. The next time she was well south of the city, she visited the Cattaraugus County Sheriff's Office with her paper napkin, now secure in a plastic bag.

"Sheriff Donaldson retired five years ago. He moved somewhere in Florida," the man now sitting at the sheriff's desk told her. "Can I help you?"

When she finished her story, the new sheriff looked at her as though she had lost her mind.

"Forget about it lady. I very much doubt you can pull DNA from a paper napkin that never touched her mouth. I may be wrong, but I'm certainly not going to ask for permission to exhume any baby's body, even if we knew where it was. And I'm really not going to pull the wonderful Mrs. Cooper into this discussion. Do you know that she is contributing most of the money for an outdoor skating rink in Olean? Why not go home and solve a mystery along with Lieutenant Columbo?"

Chapter 19
THE NEW YORK STATE CALENDAR
1983

In October 1983, Mike called Nina at the office. "Hey, how's everything with you? It's been a long time. I still grin every time I remember our last 'encounter.' I hope you and your family are all doing well. Hey, thought I would let you know that I'm going to be spending a few days in your end of the world next month on assignment. It would be great to see you."

"Hey, Mike, it's great to hear your voice. It's been a long time. What a nice surprise. What's new in your life? When are you going to be here?"

"In a couple of weeks; the publishers haven't nailed down the exact dates. Whenever it is, it sure would be great if we could cross paths. I've often thought of calling you since my second marriage fell apart."

"I'm sorry to hear about your marriage. I think about you sometimes and wonder how you're doing."

They spent the next ten minutes catching up on everything but the existence of Jennifer, who was now a Columbia Law School freshman. If Nina mentioned her and if Mike asked how old she was, Nina felt he might be suspicious.

A small voice of common sense in Nina's head was sending warning signals to let bygones be bygones, but she was not listening. As the conversation went on, she felt that old spark at the sound of his voice.

"Could we get together for a drink when I'm in town?" he asked.

"I don't know," she said, ignoring her pounding heart. "Let me think about this. I know what I should say. I also know what I want to say," she admitted.

"Let me know when you know the dates. I can sometimes get away from the office for a few hours," she said, ending the conversation.

A few weeks later, Andy, long the paper's art and architecture reporter, was on an assignment about a New York State calendar to be issued for 1985. That same calendar was the reason Mike was coming to town. He was the photographer for the entire project, which had begun months earlier at the Statue of Liberty. The calendar would have a photo of Niagara Falls and one of the statue. The other ten pictures would be taken around the state. New York State residents had been asked to vote for the other ten locations from a field of twenty-five.

Andy called Nina at the office that afternoon.

"Am I right in thinking we're not doing anything special tomorrow night?" he asked. "I just met an interesting photographer on this calendar assignment. He used to work at the *Gazette*, although I have no memory of him. He will still be in town over the weekend. I'd like to invite him for dinner tomorrow."

"Who is this man? Where did you meet him?" she asked, with a strong suspicion that she knew exactly who the photographer was.

"This guy has the contract to take the pictures for that calendar I was telling you about. He shot the New York City, Long Island and Hudson Valley pictures in the summer. He's shooting Western New York now that the leaves have turned bright colors. We got to talking. He said he remembers you."

Nina gulped.

Andy continued, "Actually, I already invited him and gave him directions to our house. I knew you wouldn't mind. I told him to come at six tomorrow night. He has a rental car. It will be fun to talk about old times at the paper. He seems like a really nice guy."

"Okay," Nina said. "It will be an interesting evening," adding to herself, "in many ways." When she hung up, Nina's heart flipped like a pancake on a hot griddle. She began to calm down a little only when she realized that if Mike had let on just how well he remembered Nina, Andy never would have invited him for dinner.

She had never cooked for Mike. In spite of herself, she was excited by the prospect. She wanted it to be a nice, homey meal. She'd make a pot roast, twice baked potatoes and her grandmother's recipe for chocolate pie. She would get most of the cooking done tonight so Andy and Mike wouldn't have much time to talk while she was in the kitchen. She would try to keep a tight control on the conversation. She planned never to look Mike straight in the eye. She would wear her new black turtleneck sweater and black skirt. She wasn't heavy but the black would make her look thinner.

The next night, Mike arrived right on time. Andy, introduced him to Nina, asking if they remembered each other.

"Of course, I remember you," Nina announced. "We were both part of that group that used to go to the Worth Hotel, next to the *Gazette*, for drinks on Saturday evenings."

"Yep. I remember," said Mike. "Those evenings at the Worth were fun. Nice to see you again. What happened to all those people? I still get Christmas cards from Bob Wallace and Ron Wysbecki. Bob went to Cleveland and became managing editor of the *Plain Dealer*. Ron went to work for the *New York Daily Mirror*. When that folded, he joined his father-in-law's auto dealership. I hear he's thriving."

Nina started to breathe again. They were on safe ground.

"I guess that was before my time," Andy said. "Or maybe I just didn't like the Worth. It was an old and creepy building. Was Steve Holden part of that group? He's still here. He's now city editor of the *Gazette*. We also get a card every year from Dean Michaels. He's in public relations for some big insurance firm in New York."

When Andy went into the kitchen to get the cocktail shaker, Mike looked at her, grinned and winked. He said not a word.

"Tell us about you and life in the big city," Andy asked Mike when he returned with the cocktail shaker and a bucket of ice. "Do you have kids?"

"I do," Mike said with a proud smile. "I have a son, Kevin. He's a Princeton graduate. Now he's doing public relations for Manufacturers Hanover here in New York. He's very busy, but we manage to have dinner once a week.

"I'm separated from my second wife. I guess I have a poor batting average. Her vegetarian cooking was excellent, but she lost interest in it. Then, she became a vegan. I really missed the eggs and cheese and felt hungry an hour after dinner. I used to eat a big meal at noon every day to keep from feeling as though I was starving by nine at night," he laughed. "I'd take Kevin out to eat one night a week when he was younger so missing hamburgers wouldn't become something important in his life. Marian didn't object to that, but then she got onto the water thing, insisting that since there was limited water in the world, we were washing ourselves and our clothes too often. That I couldn't take. But it wasn't really about that. I guess a marriage with no electricity is hard to keep up. We had no children together so the split was easy. So now I'm a man with one divorce and one annulment to his name. I haven't talked to her in about a year? That's me; tell me about you two."

"We've been lucky. We have two kids and Nina is a great cook," Andy volunteered. "And a great person," he hastily added. "Our oldest, Jon, graduated from Syracuse, majoring in accounting. He's working for an oil company in Texas. He comes home at Christmas and the Fourth of July. I miss him. Our daughter, Jennifer, just started law school at Columbia. She's sharing a small apartment with two other girls. I miss her too and worry about her in New York City."

"Well, if she needs advice about where to find a dentist or how to get cheap theater tickets or some such, have her call me," Mike said without missing a beat, even though this was the first he had heard of Jennifer. "I'm in the phone book."

Nina's stomach did that pancake flip again.

The evening went smoothly with Andy talking about how Buffalo had changed over the years and Mike talking about some of his more interesting jobs.

After Mike left, Andy commented, "I really like that

man. What an interesting and likable guy he is. We should stay in touch and call him next time we're in New York."

Nina said "yes" hoping she sounded enthusiastic.

Mike called her at the office first thing the next Monday morning.

"Hey, that was a delightful evening. What a nice dinner. The calendar folks switched the dates on me at the last minute, which is why I didn't give you notice before coming to town. I certainly enjoyed meeting Andy and hearing about your two kids. Thank you again."

Then his tone changed. "I'm sure you'll agree that our get-together for a drink while I am in town should be cancelled. It's one thing to enjoy time with the wife of someone you don't know. Now that I've met Andy, you and I getting together would be wrong. He's a really nice guy. I couldn't do that to him.

"I couldn't turn down his dinner invitation though. I wanted to see you in your home. I'm really happy for you and more than a little jealous of your family life."

Less than a week later, Andy announced that he had dropped a note to Jennifer with Mike's name and phone number, and had also sent Jennifer's contact information to Mike. "All our New York friends have moved to Westchester, Jersey or Long Island. We don't know anyone in Manhattan anymore. I think it would be a good thing if Jennifer had someone to call in an emergency—and he offered."

This time, Nina made no comment.

The following Sunday, when Jennifer called home, as she did every week, she told Andy that someone named Mike O'Neill had called her and told her he was a friend of her mom and dad's. "He said you told him to look out for me. He suggested taking me to dinner so I'd get to know him and could ask him for city information if I needed it. Is he for real?"

"Yes, he's a friend of ours who was in Buffalo last week. He used to work at the *Gazette*," Andy answered. Nina on the second phone, as she always was on that weekly three-sided call, said nothing.

The following Sunday, Jennifer reported that she'd had dinner with Mike.

"He brought his son along so it would be a more interesting evening for me. I doubt I'll ever need to call Mr. O'Neill. Yet, I suppose it's good to have a friendly person with a Manhattan phone number in an emergency. Actually, dinner was fun. They gave me the names of a batch of free galleries, concerts, events and cheap places to go if I ever have a date or free time."

Jennifer rarely talked about a social life. Her parents presumed, correctly, that her first-year law school studies did not leave much time away from her books.

Chapter 20
THE SURPRISE
1986

When Andy was a boy, he often went fishing with his dad on the Red River in North Dakota. He still felt that no vacation was a real vacation if it didn't include good fishing. He convinced Nina, so each August, they would head to Canada's Muskoka Lakes. Much to her surprise, Nina grew to enjoy these trips. However, city girl that she was, she still liked the theater, the museums and the shopping in Manhattan. Andy disliked the crowds and the prices there. He went, when on assignment for unusual New York art or architectural happenings like the opening of the World Trade Center or the King Tut exhibit, but rarely for pleasure. Since meeting Mike, he would call him when he was in New York on these assignments and they would often meet for lunch. Dinners he reserved for Jennifer during her law school years there.

As an editorial writer, Nina no longer covered the New York fashion shows. However, she would go on her own for a long weekend every fall. When Jennifer was in law school there, Nina would spend time with her. Andy typically missed the trips when Nina met Jennifer in the big city, but was content to enjoy her company when she came home on school holidays.

Nina often asked Jennifer about her social life. Jennifer was always noncommittal. In fact, she had been dating

Mike's son, Kevin, since shortly after she met him at that dinner with Mike during her first year in law school. She figured (wrongly) that her parents would be so excited about her socializing with Mike's son, they would push too hard for a romance so she had decided to keep their dating to herself.

It was the 15th of February, 1986, when Jennifer made the unusual midweek telephone call home. Now in her last year in law school, she had stayed home less than a week at Christmas. She said it was just so she could interview for a job in New York. She hoped to be rehired by the small firm where she had worked as an intern the previous summer. They had given her no guarantee.

"I'm engaged," she announced to her startled parents. "To Kevin O'Neill, Mike O'Neill's son. We've been dating almost since I first met him. We plan to be married this summer, after my graduation."

Nina thought she would have a heart attack. Although she was fairly sure that Andy was Jennifer's father, she had never been absolutely certain that her spontaneous afternoon with Mike, the day of their revolving door meeting, hadn't resulted in Jennifer.

As Nina choked out congratulations, Andy rejoiced and said to Jennifer, "Great news. If the apple doesn't fall far from the tree, and I'm pretty sure it doesn't, I bet he's a very special young man. Did you know that I met Kevin once when I was having lunch in New York with Mike? I really liked him."

Nina, realizing that she hadn't sounded pleased or excited at the news, struggled to change her tone. "That is exciting but surprising. We didn't know that you were seriously involved with anyone. I'm thrilled for you, just stunned," she said. "Why didn't you tell us you were dating someone seriously?"

Jennifer said, "I was afraid you would push too hard because of your friendship with his dad."

As soon as they hung up, Nina turned to Andy and said, "I wonder if she's too young. I'm sure this is good news, but it's a real surprise."

Andy responded, "Jennifer is a bright young woman. I'm sure she's made a sensible choice."

Nina and Andy discussed the news for a few minutes. Then, Andy announced that this news deserved a drink.

"That's a good idea but the shock has given me a bad headache. We've been out of aspirin all week. I meant to pick some up yesterday, but I forgot. I'd better drive to the drugstore quickly before it closes. You mix the martinis. I'll be right back."

She ran upstairs, saying, "Where did I put the car keys?" They actually were in her purse, but she used those few seconds to find the phone book with Mike's number, writing it on a piece of paper before she left the house.

Chapter 21
THE PHONE CALL

At the drugstore, Nina raced to the pay phone in the back. With shaking hands, she dialed Mike's number. Much to Nina's dismay, Mike didn't answer his phone. Nina was so upset, she almost forgot to buy the aspirin she had used as an excuse to make the call out of earshot of Andy. She would need a new excuse to leave the house in a few hours to try a pay phone again.

She could not think of a good story that evening, so it was early the next morning on her way to work, before she stopped back at the drugstore, that she headed for the phone booth. She woke Mike. He didn't sound too cheerful as he picked up the phone.

"Mike, it's Nina. We have to talk! There's a real crisis. We've got to stop our kids' wedding. I wasn't honest with you years ago. I lied to you about my contraception the afternoon of the revolving door all those years ago. Andy and I were having trouble conceiving a second child. I wanted to be with you, of course, but I also thought that an extramarital spin might solve our second-baby problem. If it turned out that you were the father, what would be the harm? I never dreamed that something like this could happen. I think Jennifer is Andy's daughter but I'm not sure. I never wanted to know. But, there is a chance she is Kevin's half-sister," Nina blurted out.

"Just take a deep breath," Mike interrupted. "And, by

the way, it would have been nice if you had begun the conversation with 'Hello.' Calm down," Mike continued. "I've known about the kids' romance for a long time. I knew Kevin's proposal was coming. The kids called me last night with their news.

"In the first place, Kevin is not my biological son. Caitlin was pregnant with Bruce's child when we entered into our sham marriage, which, incidentally, was never consummated. Bruce's divorce hadn't come through. She felt that the quartet's reputation would be damaged if, as a single woman in the early 1950s, her pregnancy began to show when they performed, particularly before a young audience. Today, probably, no one would care. But that was then, during the postwar years when everything was about married bliss and a little home in the suburbs.

"My dad figured it out almost immediately, but Caitlin's parents were so happy in what they believed. We rented a two-bedroom apartment near their place. Caitlin rejoined the quartet when Kevin was just a few months old. When they were on the road, Kevin stayed with her folks. I was expected to take him every Sunday. When he was almost two, Caitlin's mother had a stroke. Although she recovered, she didn't feel able to take on the responsibility of a toddler. As the one who had originally claimed fatherhood of Kevin, he became my responsibility. Caitlin and Bruce were married at that point but really busy, and I have to admit I grew to love him as my son. At first, it was hard. After a couple of months, that kid and his smile won me over. I came to think that he was mine. I always introduce him as my son. The only people who know the truth are our families and Kevin. He had to know since he spent most of each summer vacation with his 'real' parents.

"I was earning enough by that point to pay for his day care. I fixed my schedule so that much of the time, I would work only four days a week. The lucky kid always had his Colorado vacation when the streets of New York were steaming. Kevin has known the true story for years. Secondly, I've suspected I might be Jennifer's father since the day I had dinner at your house and first learned of her existence. You had never mentioned her. That evening, Andy showed me the picture of his *two* children. When I asked how old they were, the math and your secrecy made me wonder. Fortunately for many reasons, Jennifer looks like you. There's no hint of me in her looks.

"Kevin and Jennifer will have a great marriage. They're wonderful kids. I've met Jennifer often at Sunday dinners with Kevin. I could wish nothing better for that young man. Hey, if Jennifer is mine and if they ever have children, I could really be a biological grandfather. I might want to do a new DNA test but the results wouldn't affect anything."

"Whoa," Nina said, breathing normally for the first time since Jennifer's phone call the night before. "Thank God! I can breathe again. I can't believe you suspected and never said anything.

"By the way, if you do DNA testing, promise you'll never tell me the results. I don't ever want to know. I don't believe we ever wrote letters or took pictures, but someday, maybe, when we're both long gone, something might come up. The kids might learn the story and jump off a bridge. Can you make sure Kevin accepts the fact that you're not his biological father, something he would surely share with Jennifer? Then, just in case news about our old relationship surfaces someday, they won't panic. Secrets can surface inconveniently. Suppose she someday has a kid who looks like you? For Jennifer's sake and her adoration of her father, I don't suppose they ever need to know about our relationship," Nina said.

A week later, Mike called Nina at work. "This time, I'll start the conversation with a 'Hello. How are you?' which is what you should have done when you woke me up in your panic last week. The kids had dinner here the other night and I took Jennifer's water glass and had her DNA tested. I am *not* Jennifer's father. You said you never wanted to know, but I think you should know. The man who walks Jennifer down the aisle will not only be the father who raised her but also her biological father, unless you picked someone else up on the street that week," he said with an evil grin.

Chapter 22
TYING THE KNOT
1987

The wedding was held late that June on the lawn of the house in Rye, New York, where the parents of Jennifer's friend and college roommate, Marcy Watson, lived. Marcy was the bride's only attendant. Kevin thought of asking his friend Bill to be best man but opted for Mike instead. Rented chairs were put out in rows with an aisle up the center for the 120 guests. The weather was a perfect 75 degrees. Jennifer looked beautiful in a knee-length, fitted, sleeveless, white dress. She wore a wreath of daisies in her hair and carried a bouquet to match. She was festive, but not formal.

Because of the relative informality of the wedding, Andy won out in a small family discussion. He was allowed to escort his daughter down the aisle in his beloved cowboy boots. However, Nina and Jennifer had insisted he get a pair that were not scuffed.

At the rehearsal dinner the night before the wedding, Nina spotted an attractive, slim, red-haired woman about her age. She guessed correctly that this was Caitlin, Kevin's mother. The tall, equally slim man with her had to be Bruce. Just to be sure, she asked Jennifer who the couple was.

"They are Kevin's real parents. It's a long story that I won't go into now," Jennifer answered. "I'll introduce you and Dad later."

Nina let out a deep breath. If anything about her past relationship with Mike came up in the future—and she hoped it never would—Jennifer would know Kevin's true parentage.

There had long been an unspoken rivalry between Mike, Caitlin and Bruce where Kevin was concerned. Caitlin and Bruce, who had been teaching in Aspen until two days before the ceremony, flew in along with the cellist and violist from their quartet so that they could play at the wedding. Kevin was the only child among the four musicians. They'd all watched him grow up during those Colorado summers.

The wedding weekend turned out to be even more of a happy occasion for Nina and Andy. After the rehearsal dinner, Jennifer's older brother, Jon, who had arrived earlier in the day with his wife, Cindy, and their young daughter, Leslie, drew his parents aside.

"Cindy and I are leaving Texas. I am opening an accounting office in Boston with my old business school buddy, Tom. Leslie is still very young, but we don't want her going to school in Texas. I'll be a lot closer to you guys too. You'll see us more often. Anyway, it's time. If I'm ever going into business, it should be now. Tom has been living and working in Boston since he moved there right after graduation. It's not the stuffy city it once was. It's full of young people making good salaries who are sure to need help with taxes and estate planning."

Nina and Andy could not have been happier that day.

At the wedding, Mike and Nina were rarely alone with each other. However, there were a few moments, when Andy went to talk to Jennifer. It was then that Mike whispered to Nina, "I see your dad, but I don't see your mother here. I take it she is no longer alive or is unable to travel? Or, is she staying home because it is an interfaith wedding?"

"She died last year," Nina said. "If she were here, I think she would be frowning, not screaming. Times have changed. I suspect her friends' grandchildren have been intermarrying for years. It's no longer very unusual."

Mike looked at Nina in her simple blue dress and wondered, not for the first time, if he had made a serious mistake years back. Certainly, his life would have been less lonely after Kevin grew up. Then again, he remembered that if had stayed with Nina, Kevin would never have entered his life in the first place.

Nina, holding tight to her husband's hand, had no regrets. Nonetheless, she admired the way Mike looked in his blue jacket, white button-down shirt and khaki slacks.

Chapter 23
BACK TO BETTY

It was a Sunday morning, three months later, back in Western New York. The *Buffalo Gazette* had become a seven-day-a-week paper, and Andy, looking at it over his second cup of coffee, let out a gasp.

"Oh my God. Look at this," he said as he handed the paper to Nina.

The headline read: "Board Ousts President of Cooper's Markets." The story explained that Betty Cooper had inherited the markets six years back, when her husband died. It quoted one board member, who declined to be identified by name, saying the board had, over the years, found Mrs. Cooper to be intractable.

"She thought we were kindergartners and she was the teacher. She refused to listen to anyone else's ideas. Some of her own ideas simply were too costly to implement in today's highly competitive grocery market."

Two months later, there was another *Gazette* headline: "Entrepreneur Killed in Car Crash." The story said that Betty Cooper, who had recently been ousted as president of the chain of Cooper's supermarkets, had driven off a shoreline road into Lake Erie on a clear night. She left no known survivors. When the company's general counsel, who still handled Betty's ownership interest in the company, went with the police to her home, they found what looked like a suicide note.

"No longer any reason to get up in the morning" was all it said.

Betty Cooper, it turned out, had left her considerable estate in its entirety to a fund she had set up the year before: *The Brenda Roeder Foundation for College Scholarships in Marketing.* Roeder, the story said, was her maiden name.

"Maybe she is remembering her mother," Andy surmised. "If she did kill that baby, as you have believed for all these years, you can finally put that whole case out of your mind."

"Betty was two years younger than me. Her mother must have been born in the first decade of the twentieth century. I don't think anyone was named Brenda then. I'll bet the foundation is named for the dead baby," Nina said.

"You just can't let that story go, can you? Well, you'll never be able to prove anything. Since the poor woman is now dead, can you please just forget it?" Andy said. "It's a sad story and you'll never really know the truth."

Chapter 24
THE SHOCKING NEWS
1987

Andy and Nina were both still working at the *Gazette*. They enjoyed what they did and saw no point in retiring. By that time, they were each entitled to four weeks of annual vacation, enough time for Andy's annual fishing trip and time to visit Jon's family in Boston, Jennifer and Kevin in New York and still have a week to take care of their house and garden. Their trips usually lasted three days except for the time years back when Jon had married fellow accountant Cindy MacGregor, a Texan by birth, who at the time worked for the same firm Jon did. The only other long trip was when the Conway's blonde, blue-eyed granddaughter, Leslie was born.

Andy and Nina were delighted to be grandparents. While they hadn't minded visiting Texas, Nina was definitely happier on the summer trips after Jon and Cindy had moved to Boston.

Unfortunately, the summer of '86 was an unusually hot one in New England. On that summer's trip, Andy had wilted in the August heat. Every day had seen the mercury rise above 90 degrees and the humidity was worse. Andy seemed to recover his energy once he returned home.

It came as a total shock, six months later, when Andy suffered a fatal heart attack while shoveling heavy snow in his Clarence home driveway.

Jennifer, Jon and Cindy flew to Buffalo immediately. Kevin flew in the next day along with Mike, who called as soon as he heard the news.

"If you're having friends speak at the service, please include me. I didn't meet Andy until we worked on that calendar together, but our New York lunches and our letters were a real pleasure to me. I will miss that man. And Nina," he said, "if sometimes you want to cry, but not in front of your friends or children, I'm just a phone call away. That's what old, out-of-town pals are for. I'll always be there for you."

Chapter 25
THE CAPE
1988

That August, Jon, Cindy, Jennifer and Kevin rented a beach house on Cape Cod for a week. It was on Melbourne Road in West Hyannisport. They persuaded Nina to come along. It was an old house about a half a mile from the beach.

"Sun and shore are good for everyone," Jon said. "You'll get quality time with your granddaughter and with us. There's no reason not to come."

What they didn't tell Nina was that they had also invited Mike, as long as he would be willing to sleep on the screened porch. Kevin and Jennifer suggested the plan. They all agreed that since Mike and Nina had spent time at the Buffalo paper, they would have old times and colleagues to talk about.

After some convincing, Nina finally agreed to join them and flew to Boston, driving to the Cape with Jon, Cindy and baby Leslie. They met Kevin, Jennifer and Mike, who had arrived a day earlier, at the house. Nina was shocked when she realized Mike was there too. Nonetheless, her heart did a little old flutter although she was still missing Andy every day. She and Mike exchanged only polite conversation that first evening.

Early the next morning, Jon, Jennifer and Kevin decided to go for a run on the beach. Cindy stayed in to watch Leslie.

Nina said, "If it's all right with you, I'll go along. I'll walk while you run. I'll go a shorter distance than you young ones but we can all meet back at the car."

Kevin turned to Mike, who was engrossed in the James Patterson murder mystery he had brought along. "Why don't you come too? A walk will do you good." Mike put down the book, seemingly with reluctance and agreed to go. He walked with Nina along the beach, never having been into running.

When he and Nina were out of earshot from the runners, he smiled and said, "It's so good to see you, Nina. I know you've had a tough year. I think about you so often. The kids didn't tell you in advance that I was coming, because they knew it was too soon for what, I think, they hope will lead to a match between two aging singles."

Without another word, they both grinned.

After a bit of small talk, Nina said, "The day of the wedding, after I was introduced to Caitlin and Bruce, Jen said to me: 'They are Kevin's real parents. I don't know the whole story, but I guess Mike adopted him. Kevin certainly has been an important part of Mike's life and total joy to him.' Jen does not know that I know the real story," continued Nina. "I don't know if she needs to. Her remarks that day took a weight off my mind.

"She need never know that her ethical mother cheated on the dad she so adored. As you and I discussed before the kids were married, you never know what might come to light someday, maybe after we're long gone. I hope nothing does, but if it does, they'll know that she and Kevin are definitely not biologically related."

"I've sometimes wondered what our lives would have

been like if you had moved to New York with me when I left the newspaper," Mike mused.

"It wouldn't have worked," Nina said. "In competitive New York, I would never have built the career that I've had. I would have ended up frustrated and angry. Furthermore, I wasn't ready to settle down. I suspect you weren't either. Besides, it was a time when what parents thought meant so much more than it does now. Plus, grandparents and family holidays in Buffalo gave a great deal of stability to my kids as they grew up. They would have missed out on that. We definitely took the right paths back then."

"You may or may not be right," Mike said. "But that was then. I've often wondered why it took me so long to remarry and if one of the reasons my marriage to Marian failed was because I have always been in love with you. This is now. Why go home every day to an empty house? Your kids have grown and moved away. Something about that electricity between us, right from day one, has never gone away. Of course, I know that you are still mourning Andy, but I hope you don't get too used to living alone."

Then, Mike said something that startled Nina.

"Think about coming to New York and staying with me. Maybe just come for a weekend or two—or three. We've never spent a few days alone together. If our relationship works out, I can think of no happier thought than having you move in and stay. After all, the years go by too quickly.

"Sure, you have a good job but you've been at the *Gazette* for thirty-eight years. The job can't mean as much to you as it did in the beginning. You would be closer to Jennifer and Kevin, and to Jon, Cindy and Leslie as well. What's equally important, we would be together. If we are lucky, we've still got twenty or more years ahead of us.

Why spend them alone? If you think it is too soon, we can wait until you think the time is right. The lights for me have always burned most brightly when we've been together.

"I've been giving the matter a lot of thought since the kids told me they had invited us both up here. I know you would never be happy just staying at home, although from a financial point of view, I can support you in any style you like. Think about what we could do. We could publish a book together, your words and my photos. You could volunteer at the Metropolitan Museum or the Museum of Modern Art or one of the hundreds of galleries in the city. I'm sure you learned a great deal living with an art reporter all those years. You might even be able to get a part-time public relations job. If you didn't want to work, we would be free to travel together on my more interesting assignments. If Jennifer and Kevin ever decide to have kids, you could be an occasional babysitter and watch your grandchild or grandchildren grow up. Our love life might not be as exciting as when we were younger, but I'd sure like to find out.

"Maybe we wouldn't get along on an everyday basis, though somehow I doubt that. But right now, I can't look at you for two minutes without wanting to hold you."

With that, he drew her close and kissed her. She kissed him back.

"It's been a long time," he said. "I've been divorced from Marian for years."

"Life would be better with you than without you," Nina said, more quickly than she might have. Then she added, "What would people think? Andy hasn't been gone a year. I miss him every day. What would the kids think?"

"The kids would think they made the match. They told me you were coming to the Cape. They didn't tell you because they knew, with your sense of propriety, you wouldn't come. If we decided to live together, they would be proud of themselves. We would never need to mention our history.

"I'd love to move off that damned screen porch tonight, but I won't. In the fall, come visit me in New York for a few weekends. Let's see how things go.

"Whether or not you like my scenario, we'd better walk back a little faster. Even though the kids' run is longer than our walk, I don't want them to think that a big wave washed us away."

They walked in silence for a few minutes.

"I don't know," Nina finally said. "For a long time I've believed that I loved both you and Andy."

Mike responded, "Whatever you decide, here's a plan. Let's offer to sit with Leslie some night this week. The kids can go to dinner or a movie or both. I think they would trust us to watch the little one, particularly if she's asleep. That's just a nice thing to do.

"Think about what I'm saying. I doubt that Andy would have wanted you to be alone for the rest of your life. If it works out after those weekends and if your concern then is that your friends will think it's too soon, tell them you're moving to New York because that is where Jennifer and Kevin live. Tell them that you need a change of scenery."

Nina paused and then declared, "That is an appealing offer. My dad used to quote some ancient Roman who said: 'He who hesitates is lost.' I have never been one to worry about what others think. I'll come for a weekend in September. Maybe we'll discover that we can't spend more than a few hours together. Who knows?"

They kissed again and walked back to the car as quickly as they could.

Secrecy had so long been a part of their relationship, it was now second nature. They mostly tried to ignore each other as the week went on. When Nina suggested babysitting Leslie so the two young couples could have an evening out, they invited Mike to come along with them. He declined, saying he wanted to finish his book. Jennifer, who had noticed he had already finished the book that afternoon, said nothing.

Cindy gave Leslie dinner and put her to bed before the four young people left for their evening out. Not ten minutes after they had gone, Mike had his arms around Nina and maneuvered her into her bedroom.

"Bet the great Mike O'Neill never made love to a fifty-year-old woman before," Nina quipped.

"Ho. She is a sixty-one-year-old woman," he retorted. "But, there is always a first time," he said with his Cheshire Cat grin. "Our relationship was always great physically. I still feel lust when I look at you. I want you in my bed. I want you in my house. I want you in my life."

"Wow," Nina said. "Those are the most romantic sentences I ever heard." She paused, then added, "But I have to think about it. So, for a little longer, let's stay secretive about any relationship. Let's see how things go. I'll come to New York and stay with you for a weekend next month. Maybe things will be wonderful. Maybe not. You're right. Over all these years, we have never spent a whole weekend together alone."

"Age might make a difference. Coming out of the shadows shouldn't," Mike answered.

Later that evening, when the kids came home, Mike was sitting with his open book and Nina was reading a magazine. The week flew by pleasantly. When departing, they all agreed that returning to the Cape the following year was an excellent idea. Jennifer and Kevin exchanged glances and smiled.

Chapter 26
NEW YORK

Two weeks later, right after Labor Day, Mike called Nina in Buffalo and announced:

"I've decided our first weekend together should not be in my shabby apartment. It should be wonderful. I'm hoping you will like my plan. I've made a reservation for two nights toward the end of this month at The Beekman Arms, a two-hundred-year-old inn in Rhinebeck, just up the Hudson River.

"There are the Roosevelt and Vanderbilt mansions nearby and the Culinary Institute is not too far, just in case we decide to leave our room. I've given up my car in favor of taxis in the city. I rent one when I have to leave town. I'll pick you up at LaGuardia. Let me know when you know your flights. If you already have plans for that weekend, change them."

Nina had given Mike's Cape Cod romantic remarks a lot of thought. While still unsure about a major move, she had decided that a "test drive" weekend sounded exciting. She paused for effect, and then said, "I'll come. I'll make my reservations tomorrow morning."

That first weekend was a great success. As they parted at the airport, Mike said, "Incidentally, if my hopes are realized and you decide to move to New York, you can redecorate my apartment to your heart's desire. Bring up favorite furnishings from your Clarence house if it makes you feel more at home. I know I've let things slide in terms of decor. No, not slide. They were pretty tacky from day one. For you, I'd be delighted to do a whole apartment makeover."

On her second trip to New York, the third weekend in October, Nina dropped off her luggage at Mike's place. Then, he asked her to accompany him to Zabar's on Broadway so they could pick out dinner for a night in. When they got back to Mike's apartment, he unlocked the door and told Nina, "Wait a minute. I want to pick you up and carry you over the threshold. It may be an old superstition, but I think it stands as a commitment to being a couple for the rest of our lives. We may not be making a commitment to God or to the State of New York at this time, but I'm making one to you. Anytime you want to do the legal thing, I'm ready. My divorce has long been final. To others, this may look like a whirlwind romance, but we know better."

"You're right about that spark," Nina said. "But you're dead wrong about the threshold thing. I suspect you saw it in a movie and an old one at that. I hope you realize you are about to commit to a modern woman. Carrying a bride over the doorway, like carrying in the groceries, is not a thing today. It equates her with luggage. I am sure you mean well, but it has out-of-date connotations. I know you meant it as a romantic gesture, but no thank you. If we or the IRS decide it makes sense to make our arrangement legal at a later date, that's okay with me. But not now. It's too soon."

She paused and then continued, "I expect I will be a woman who looks back at her older years as being as happy as her younger ones."

"And I'll be a man who considers them the best years of his life," Mike added. With that, he walked into his kitchen and pulled from his refrigerator the bottle of champagne that had been chilling.

"Here's to the 1950 November snowstorm that made everyone else late for work and introduced you to me. Here's to that long car ride."

"You would have met me eventually," Nina said. "As I recall, there were only six photographers at the paper. We would have been sent on the same assignment sooner or later. So, you can raise a glass to that trip; I would like to toast that second snowstorm when we had to share that hotel room in Arcade."

"I suppose we should raise our glasses in memory of that baby in the pumpkin shell too. That story gave us something to talk about."

"Oh!" Nina exclaimed, "I forgot to tell you! The matter has been resolved, at least in my mind. It only took thirty-eight years. I'll tell you all about it over dinner." Then seeing the look on Mike's face, she added, "But maybe not tonight." And with that she stepped into Mike's open arms.

Epilogue

It was a weekend in late November. Nina had given notice at the *Gazette* and was preparing to sell the Clarence house. She and Mike were no longer hiding their relationship.

That Sunday afternoon, they were walking in Central Park, enjoying the sight of the last colorful autumn leaves and the crunchy sound they made under foot. Without thinking about it, they were holding hands. When they heard rapidly approaching footsteps behind them on the footpath, they turned and saw a young couple catching up to them, the young woman at a faster pace than the young man.

"Excuse me," she said as soon as she reached them. "From the way you two walk, holding hands, you look like people who've been married for a very long time and are still in love. Ted and I are engaged. My parents have been divorced for years and so have Ted's. What's your secret?"

Neither Mike nor Nina was about to tell her that they hadn't been living together for thirty years or even thirty days. They were both silent for a minute. Then Mike spoke.

"Patience," he said with a smile.

Then he and Nina walked on.

About Atmosphere Press

Atmosphere Press is an independent, full-service publisher for excellent books in all genres and for all audiences. Learn more about what we do at atmospherepress.com.

We encourage you to check out some of Atmosphere's latest releases, which are available at Amazon.com and via order from your local bookstore:

The Hidden Life, a novel by Robert Castle
Big Beasts, a novel by Patrick Scott
Alvarado, a novel by John W. Horton III
Nothing to Get Nostalgic About, a novel by Eddie Brophy
GROW: A Jack and Lake Creek Book, a novel by Chris S McGee
Home is Not This Body, a novel by Karahn Washington
Whose Mary Kate, a novel by Jane Leclere Doyle
Stuck and Drunk in Shadyside, a novel by M. Byerly
These Things Happen, a novel by Chris Caldwell
Vanity: Murder in the Name of Sin, a novel by Rhiannon Garrard
Blood of the True Believer, a novel by Brandann R. Hill-Mann
The Glorious Between, a novel by Doug Reid
An Expectation of Plenty, a novel by Thomas Bazar
Sink or Swim, Brooklyn, a novel by Ron Kemper

About the Author

Sue Buyer was graduated from Vassar, then a women's college, in 1947. After a summer at the University of Zurich, she returned stateside and worked for several years in secretarial jobs. With encouragement from her then-boss, she attended the Columbia School of Journalism, where women comprised fewer than 10% of the class. Upon graduation, she went to work at *The Buffalo Evening News*, where she remained for 27 years, and married a fellow reporter. Fast forward to the present, she recalled her newsroom experiences to write this story. She currently lives and writes in Western New York.